D0922935

THE LIBERAL PARTY

THE MEN AND IDEAS SERIES
III

General Editor: R. W. Harris
*Master of Studies and Head of the History Department,
the King's School, Canterbury*

THE FIRST THREE VOLUMES:

TUDOR ECONOMIC PROBLEMS
by Peter Ramsey
Lecturer in History, the University of Bristol

POLITICAL IDEAS 1760–1792
by R. W. Harris

THE LIBERAL PARTY FROM
EARL GREY TO ASQUITH
by R. B. McCallum

THE MEN AND IDEAS SERIES
III

THE LIBERAL PARTY FROM EARL GREY TO ASQUITH

by

R. B. McCALLUM

Master of Pembroke, Oxford

LONDON
VICTOR GOLLANCZ LTD
1963

PRINTED IN GREAT BRITAIN
BY EBENEZER BAYLIS AND SON, LTD.
THE TRINITY PRESS, WORCESTER, AND LONDON

DEDICATION

To the memory of my father, Andrew
McCallum, Master Dyer, of Paisley, who
brought me up in Liberal thought, always
taking pains to tell me about the other side
of the question.

CONTENTS

ONE

THE REFORM BILL AND ITS CONSEQUENCES

THE POLITICAL SPIRIT which in Great Britain is known as Liberal is by no means new. If we take the years 1830 to 1832 as a starting-point, we will find it to be a rational dividing line. In these years there took place throughout the country a memorable struggle, a contest that was fought in Parliament, in any place where men debated and discussed, in the streets and at the polling places. There were two general elections and there were dangerous riots and commotions: Nottingham Castle was burned down, the centre of Bristol given over to riot, pillage and arson. In the learned reviews and serious newspapers there was argument at a high intellectual level; there was a run on the gold reserves of the Bank of England; there was pressure on the throne and pressure by the throne. And this struggle was centred on one particular measure, a Bill before Parliament which became eventually an Act. And nearly all men, according to their education and understanding, knew what the struggle was about. It was about the franchise, the right to vote for members of the House of Commons, the constituencies in which electors could vote and the degree of freedom and effectiveness with which this vote could be exercised. Politicians would argue with sinuous skill about forty shilling freeholds, about ancient right voters, about the effect of ending the so-called rotten or closed boroughs, about the desirability of having a register of electors. Some bold spirits even spoke of vote by ballot, secret voting. In the streets the Reform mobs had their simple slogan, their one appealing cry, "The Bill, the whole Bill and nothing but the Bill."

It seemed to many, and it was no fantastic nightmare, that the country was on the verge of revolution and civil war. This was averted; it was only just averted by the firmness of the ministry in power, by the prudence of the Lords when faced with the royal prerogative of creating Peers to carry the Bill. It was averted also by the comparative tranquillity of London, where Sir Robert Peel's new Metropolitan Police had just been installed. When the dust had settled and a new Parliament had been elected the country settled down to a period of peaceful and moderate change.

The new Parliament had an immense majority of a party that was becoming slowly to be called Liberal, just as its opponents were to be called Conservative. From this time on the people were to be accustomed to having before them, not indeed two firmly organised political phalanxes such as we know now, but two distinctive groups of which the one was the party of change and experiment, the other the party of conservation and resistance to all but the most necessary change. The parties fought the reform fight under their old names, which continued in use for some decades, the names of Whig and Tory. For the dispute which had crystallised round this one measure, the reform of the Parliamentary system, was not entirely new. The parties with these names had been before the country for a century and a half.

Since the year 1641 the people of England, politically speaking, have been in schism. In that year the famous Long Parliament which King Charles I had been forced to summon to sustain him in his quarrel with the Scottish Presbyterian Covenanters, itself divided. At first the Members had worked with some agreement to restrain the powers of the Crown and to remove what they considered to be abuses. But the zealots in the Parliament went further and attacked the Church of England; they had no trust and confidence in the King, whose advisers to them had the air of sinister tyrants. We know how the House divided over a document called the Grand Remonstrance, how the minority, who deemed their loyalty to the King to be paramount, left London with him, how the majority, with the rump of the Lords, remained in London and waged civil war against their sovereign. They did this in many names, law, liberty and pure religion, by which was meant the Protestant religion in what was deemed to be its purest form. The classic form of this was that in which it had been cast by John Calvin, the great Doctor of Geneva, whose noble eloquence and lucid perfection of thought affected men's minds as by a revelation. We know, however, that to many of the most ardent minds amongst the Parliamentary side there was too much of an orthodoxy in this; they leaned to more individual forms of belief and worship; they renounced the classic system for another ideal, the Independent or Congregational ideal. Under the inspired leadership of Cromwell and his captains, this faction within a party prevailed; it set its yoke on all three kingdoms until, with the death of its great leader, it collapsed.

When peace and the King were restored, there was an upsurge of Cavalier and Anglican loyalty which seemed to carry all before it. But the schism of 1641 had not been healed. When opposition to the Court and Government of the restored King dared to manifest itself, the dividing line between the opposing factions, hazy as it was, seemed to be determined most of all by the antecedents of the younger generation, whose fathers had known the Civil War. John Locke, the son of a Somerset Captain in the Parliamentary Army, became the philosopher of the Whigs, the defender and advocate of government by consent, the apostle of that measured liberty which is prized on both sides of the Atlantic. Ashley-Cooper, Lord Shaftesbury, who held commands in the Parliamentary Army and later aided in the Restoration and held office under Charles II, became the Leader of the Opposition and the founder of the Whig party, the demoniac figure described in Dryden's *Absalom and Achitophel*. The Civil War had been partly a religious war,

partly social and partly purely political. The fundamental
political idea which the Parliamentarians handed down to
their successors, who were later to be known as Whigs, was
that ultimate political authority rested not with the Crown
or in any hereditary person but was under some form of
limitation, subject to some form of consent, transmuted
through whatever organs by whatever means ascertained.
This school of thought rejected the notion that all resistance
to established royal authority was illegal and wicked. It
reserved some ultimate right to resist. This right was
exercised in the Revolution of 1688, a revolution carried out
by both Whig and Tory leaders, horrified as they were by
the illegality and the papistry of King James II. Probably
the majority of the people, including the all-important
nobility and gentry, were in sentiment Tories. But the Tories
were divided into those who could accept the rule of William
and Mary, and later of Queen Anne, and those who were
Jacobites and could work only for a Stuart Restoration. The
Whig ideas triumphed in the acts of the revolution settlement,
the Bill of Rights of 1688, the Act of Settlement of 1701.
When the Protestant succession of the House of Hanover
was successfully accomplished the Whigs were the beneficiaries; power and wealth and rank were theirs and in due
course, with the waning of Jacobitism, they became a sated
and possessing party, and by 1760 little difference might be
detected between men who gave themselves the different
party names.

But the differences were there. The old traditions were
not dead and the American Revolution posed the question
of authority versus consent in a challenging form. Many
men of Whig antecedents concurred in the ministerial
policies which brought about the war and supported the
Government. Others in varying degrees doubted the wisdom
and justice of the struggle and withheld approval and support.
It was left to Whig ministers to make peace with the colonies
and with France and at the same time to make some notable

concessions to the constitutional demands of the Irish Protestants for Parliamentary freedom. The French Revolution and the long struggle with Napoleon's military despotism reduced the power of Whigs to a low ebb. Charles James Fox, the greatest of the Whig statesmen, did his best to see good and hope in the events of France but Edmund Burke, the deepest thinker of the party, took the other side and became with his famous *Reflections on the French Revolution* the leading apostle of European conservatism. Throughout the war and for fifteen years after Pitt and his followers, now styled Tories, had undisputed control of Parliament and the fundamental support of the political nation. The small Whig remnant was weak and divided. But with the coming of peace it found leaders. It found growing support in certain circles. There were a few of the noble families who were centred on Holland House, the home of Fox's nephew, Lord Holland. Charles Grey, now Earl Grey, a former friend of Fox was the nominal leader. In the Commons and amongst the professional classes support grew. There were lawyers like Romilly, fighting barristers like Brougham, afterwards Lord Chancellor, brilliant wits and writers like the Rev. Sydney Smith and young Thomas Babington Macaulay, young patricians also like Lord John Russell of the Bedford family. And they had their mouthpiece in journalism in the *Edinburgh Review* which became for a time one of the most brilliant in Europe. It expounded not exactly a creed, for the Whig or Liberal thought of the time was flexible and varied, not exactly a doctrine, but rather a critical and searching spirit which examined the problems and institutions of the day unprejudiced in favour of what was ancient and established and at the same time without swallowing the nostrums of whole-hogging radicals and systematic theorists like the utilitarians.

For beyond the orthodox practising Whigs and Liberals, the men of good formal education, the men who could aspire to Parliament and office, there was a broad belt of political thought to which the general name Radical was given. There were philosophic radicals like the writer James Mill and his more remarkable son John Stuart, disciples of the famous Jeremy Bentham who died in the month of the great Reform Bill. They applied the hard and searching test of utility and the happiness of the greater number to all political and social problems. They were to be what we might now call "the back-room boys" of political reform. They were then few, a sect or a coterie, but their influence was to grow until it informed the thought of most educated Englishmen. Then there were radicals of the kind called "sentimental" such as William Cobbett whose *Political Register* had been a force in the land, men of no theory or system but with a firm belief in the worth and right of the common man. Others like Francis Place, the political tailor, influenced both practising politicians and the humbler classes by a straightforward political radicalism. Then, on a very different plane was O'Connell, the great Irish tribune and orator, who had won with Whig support the fight for Catholic emancipation and who had a following in Parliament elected for Irish constituencies whose aim was Repeal of the union, what was later to be called Home Rule. All these radical sections were appeased or patronised with varying degrees of approval, fear and distaste by the orthodox Whigs. The open and enquiring mind of the *Edinburgh Review* Whig would not wholly dismiss these radicals as evil or worthless. But they went too far and their ideas were dangerous. They were dangerous either in that they were wrong or utterly impracticable, or they were dangerous in that they were discreditable allies, men whose support alienated more than it attracted. To let them aboard would sink the ship.

For one thing these radicals, with the exception of the Irish under O'Connell who were mostly pious Catholics, were often men of no religion, doubters, nullifidians, or, to use a word that was not yet invented, agnostics. The people of England, Scotland, Ireland and Wales in the nineteenth century were for the most part deeply religious and those who had little personal religion, unless they were of a boldly independent character, took good care outwardly to conform. Sir Robert Ensor has said in his history of England from 1870 that "among highly civilised, in contradistinction to more primitive, countries, Victorian England was one of the most religious that the world has known". And in 1832 the religious tide was flowing and not ebbing; scoffers like Melbourne were to give way to zealots like Gladstone. No party, no rational seekers after political power, could disregard the force of religion. What was the religious complexion of the Whig-Liberal party?

One thing must not be said; the Whigs must not be identified with the Protestant Dissenters or nonconformists. That is nonsense. Although from the Toleration Act of William and Mary of 1689 certain reliefs had been granted to dissenters and later by annual indemnity acts they had been permitted to hold some public offices, it was not until 1828 that with the repeal of the restrictive laws they were given full civic freedom. The Whig party could not have existed, could not have provided men of rank and wealth and consequence to lead the nation unless it had been in the main a party of members of the established church. But while the Whig party was not the party of the nonconformists it was the party for the nonconformists.[1] Its ancestry, as we have seen, was sprung from the Puritan or Presbyterian half of the Long Parliament and one of its last legal actions was to remove the Bishops from the House of Lords. When the more moderate element in the Puritan party, those who were called "presbyterians", (it was perhaps more of a political than an ecclesiastical label,) rallied to the restoration of the Crown, the wealthier and more eminent amongst them conformed to the church of England. But they had a

[1] It was not until 1868 that an English nonconformist entered the Cabinet.

conscience about their more extreme brethren who remained outside, who endured the rigours of the Clarendon Code. These dissenters had the sympathy of the Whig politicians and were also most useful allies. Thus the Whigs became the patrons of nonconformity; the nonconformists became their clients. There was however more than natural sympathy and useful alliance in this. The Whigs were in principle the party of toleration. Their great thinker Locke had advocated it. Toleration all round they could not achieve for more than a century. For there was another kind of dissenter, the Roman Catholic dissenter, who was excluded from all office by various acts of Parliament, notably the famous Test Acts of Charles II. While the Roman Catholics were Jacobites, suspected often rightly of working for a Stuart Restoration, they had to be outside the pale. But by the end of the eighteenth century the Whigs feared this danger less. Then the principle of toleration worked in favour of the Catholics and the Tory opposition was overcome partly by continued pressure in England and by O'Connell's skilful agitation in Ireland.

By 1830 when the dissenters enjoyed full rights as citizens they had become more powerful. This happened in two ways; they had become more numerous because the great movement called Methodism, led by Wesley and Whitefield, had detached large elements from the Anglican Church into what had become dissenting sects; they were becoming richer and more prosperous. In the eighteenth century many of them had prospered, they had become important as bankers, as brewers, as manufacturers and merchants. And it should be remembered that Scotsmen, at this time already very influential in the country's life, were nonconformists when they came south of the Border just as Anglicans became nonconformists north of the Border. The Scottish Presbyterians had a great zeal for education and controlled four universities. In England the dissenters were excluded from the two English universities but they had also a great zeal for education and in their own academies had seen that their children were well taught. Halévy in his *History of the English People in the Nineteenth Century* (Vol. I, p. 428), tells us that in 1811 the Dissenters claimed (it is perhaps an exaggeration) to be about two million out of a population, in England, of ten million; in the larger parishes the number of nonconformist chapels exceeded that of Anglican churches by about seven to five. He concludes, "while the nominal members of the establishment still constituted an enormous majority, the Nonconformists already equalled, if they did not exceed, the Anglicans who practised their religion." If united, this body might have become an irresistible force. But it was not united; nonconformity varied from Unitarians, Presbyterians and Congregationalists, who tended to be political and even republican in spirit, to Methodists who were less concerned with politics, more purely evangelical and conservative as a force. The Quakers, Society of Friends, were very radical in views but not in action. They abstained from "the carnal arm" they would not bear arms or forge them but they were zealous in charity and social reform.

Over this varied array the Whig leaders had to hold their umbrella, often with distaste for their narrow fanatical and "unenlightened" ideas. But they could not turn against them; they could not indeed promise to disestablish the church but they could aid in what was needed further to remove restrictions on all Dissenters. The Tories on the other hand were the High Church Party; this phrase hardly means what it does now, the Anglo-catholic party; that name was still in the future. But the Tories were the party that was strong for a strong church. They regretted, they even abhorred, the existence of these dissenting sects which threatened the political and social union of the nation. Zealous Anglicans had never really abandoned the ideal of the Clarendon Code which had this great merit that if successful it would have made the nation and the church to be one, as it was in Sweden or nearly so in many parts of

Scotland. Legal compulsion had gone and was nevermore to be advocated; but social pressure, persuasion in all forms, the advantages of a monopoly of higher education and the possession of all the more famous schools and endowments encouraged the Anglicans to think that conformity to the establishment was the natural and proper course; not to take this course seemed to argue some kind of perversity of mind, a love of singularity for which those who felt it must pay, pay in the most literal sense by building their own schools and churches, paying their own ministers and teachers. The Whig-Anglican stood out from the Tory-Anglican as an eccentric and misguided person, one in league with the Midianites without the walls of the citadel. When the Duke of Wellington's friend, the Tory Mrs. Arbuthnot, heard that her political and social rival, the Whig Lady Jersey, had been seen attending worship in a Presbyterian Meeting House she made a simple inference, "I think she must be mad."

While the great reform battle was waging we may note the general characteristics of the Whig-Liberal politician. He prided himself on his critical power, his political enlightenment. Disentangling himself from the poetic power of the later writings of Burke, he considered that all human institutions were capable of reform and that antiquity and usage themselves conferred no title to immunity from interference by state power. He was probably somewhat selfconsciously superior; he believed firmly in his own enlightenment. He was the enemy of anomalies of all kinds. He delighted when the *Edinburgh Review* attacked the ancient universities, above all when it exposed the abuses of Tory Oxford. The coagulated mass of charters, rights and customs that made up the gothic constitutions of the Borough Corporations were an object of his satire and contempt. The established Anglican Church in Ireland with its well endowed hierarchy to serve certainly not more than one eighth of the population was a favourite object of his scorn. "A good likeness", Sydney Smith is reported as saying when shown a new portrait of Lord John Russell, "A very good likeness, but perhaps not quite enough hatred of the Irish Church in it."

We speak of the Whig reformers. It must be said that Whigs were zealous for reform in very different degrees. For one thing the Ministry of Lord Grey was not entirely Whig: it had been strengthened on its formation by the inclusion of the "Canningite Tories", those who had separated from the Tories proper on the issue of Catholic Emancipation. Palmerston, the Foreign Secretary, was one of these and Melbourne, the Home Secretary, and Grant, afterwards Lord Glenelg. Lord Grey, something of a fire-brand in his Foxite youth, was now a very restrained reformer. The Whig ministry could not be said to march out of step; cabinet solidarity was on the whole maintained. But it was a regiment that marched rather in echelon with one section in advance of another. Behind the determination to carry a full scale reform of Parliament there were various motives. To some of the younger it was a matter of reason and even of some idealistic enthusiasm. To others it was more a matter of expediency; the old form of Parliament they knew could not last. It was better that they should make what change was necessary than that more radical forces should sweep more thoroughly. These Whig noblemen did not identify themselves with "the people"; they never strove for social equality. None of them was prepared to engage in the political antics which in France earned for the Duke of Orleans the name of Philippe Egalité. If they differed from the Tories who opposed a radical reform it was partly because of their general philosophy which held that govern-ment was in the long run by consent. It was also because they made a realistic appreciation of the state of the public and knew that the system must bend or break. It may be also that they lacked the bull-dog courage of the Tories of the post-Waterloo era, the men who had kept the social and governmental system going by sticking to their guns, fearing the fury of the populace less than the reproach of their own conscience.

The Cabinet worked with a curious form of division of labour. The elder and more conservative statesmen held the principal executive offices and kept the foreign relations of the country and the internal security in their hands. The main legislative task of the Government was entrusted in its details to younger and more radical members, Lord John Russell and Lord Durham, who with a small committee drew up the various Bills which were presented to Parliament for Reform. It can seldom have happened that a Prime Minister allowed his junior colleagues to take the lead so much in a matter of fundamental policy. But there was wisdom in Lord Grey's tactics. The younger men were keen, they knew what was wanted; they could best supply the need.

Many were the anxieties of the moderate Whigs about the changes they were sponsoring. Above all they feared for the character of the House of Commons. The old system was an "abuse", but how ancient, how splendid and famous it was. The unreformed Parliament had seen the country through the most terrible of tests in the great war with Napoleon. The people of England could say in the words of Chesterton's poem:

"The man who seemed to be more than man, we strained against and broke."

Not lightly was the instrument of government which had done this to be tampered with. Above all, the Whigs loved and respected the House of Commons. The Lords were now predominantly on the other side. Monarchy, the limited monarchy of their creation, they valued but tended to patronise. They saw it with no romantic or mystical eyes. Anthony Trollope describes the Whig Duke of Omnium, a fictitious but most convincing character, as taking a post at Court when his party were in office and performing the duties with distaste. Lord Amberley, the son of Lord John Russell and the father of the philosopher Bertrand Russell, was infuriated by some snub to his wife by Queen Victoria's cousin, the Duke of Cambridge and his wife, and he wrote wrathfully in his diary, "these royal *canaille* must be taught a lesson." But if anything was an Ark of the Covenant to these worldly and rather cynical men, it was the House of Commons, then as now the nerve centre and power house of the Constitution. It represented the nation, not the *profanum vulgus*, the ignorant mob, but the responsible political elements of the nation. By it and in it their greatest triumphs had been won; from it alone could good government proceed. In 1908 we find the Liberal Secretary for India, John Morley, reproving his Viceroy, Lord Minto, for speaking with contempt of "the House". "Your tone about the House of Commons produces in me a jar, such as would be produced in you by disrespectful language about the King."

It is not surprising, therefore, that even those who sought to reform the electoral system should have a weakness for the old, small, closed boroughs. It was said in their defence that they had been the means by which youth and talent could come to the House. Edmund Burke had been brought in in this way; in 1830 the brilliant young Cambridge scholar Macaulay, was "brought in" for the borough of Calne (once Pym's constituency) by the Whig magnate Lord Lansdowne. If these useful nurseries for aspiring talent were to go, entrance to the House would be left to men of wealth and presumably also of greater age, landed magnates, rich merchants, nabobs. This fear explains the extreme tenderness with which small boroughs were treated in the Bill and why small towns were given equal representation with large cities.

With every change in our representative system and with every development of party control, this foreboding has been expressed. Would none but rich men or old party men and now, Trade Union, hacks find their way to Westminster? The fear has always been false. After the election of 1945 two recent Presidents of the Oxford Union, one Conservative and one Labour, found safe seats. Recently an Oxford undergraduate of 23 has been elected. These men were respectively, a baronet, the son of a Labour Peer and the grandson of a Highland Chieftain. But it is not only the men privileged by birth who have this chance. In 1890 a young lawyer, the orphan of an elementary schoolteacher and the ward of a village cobbler, at the age of 26 won Carnarvon Boroughs, David Lloyd George. In 1929 two young socialists aged respectively, 32 and 25, entered Parliament for Welsh and Scottish constituencies, Mr. Aneurin Bevan and Miss Jennie Lee. They married each other. They knew and met Mr. Lloyd George and he had known Mr. Gladstone, who in 1832 had entered Parliament at the age of 23 with the laurels of his famous Oxford career fresh upon him. As for Macaulay, he was indeed squeezed out of Calne which was cut down to one seat and that had to go to Lord Lansdowne's son, but by 1832 he was famous and Leeds elected him. Later, on his return from India, the City of Edinburgh was proud to have him as a member. The continuity of British political life has been marvellously maintained.

But in 1830 and for two years to come all attention was centred on the anomaly of anomalies, the electoral law, the mode by which Members of the House of Commons were returned. Out of this chaos could no order be created? Out of this travesty of electoral justice could no rational system of distributing political power be found? It was in the achievement of this task, imperfectly achieved as we shall see but with a fundamental principle asserted, that what came to be known as the Liberal Party had its first real victory of consolidation and its first lease of firm parliamentary power.

Let us hear the words of some of the leaders on this issue. In 1822, Lord John Russell at the outset of his long career had expressed it thus. "If we ask the causes why a system of government so contrary to the spirit of our laws, so obnoxious to the feelings of our people, so ominous to the future prospects of the country has been adopted, we shall find the root of the evil, to lie in the defective state of our representation. The votes of the House of Commons no longer imply the general assent of the realm; they no longer carry with them the sympathies and understanding of the nation. The Ministers of the Crown after obtaining triumphant majorities in this house are obliged to have a recourse to other means than those of persuasion, reverence for authority and voluntary respect, to procure the adherence of the country. They are obliged to enforce by arms obedience to acts of this house, which according to every just theory are supposed to emanate from the people themselves."

In the Reform Bill debates in October 1831, Macaulay repeated this thesis. In December 1831, speaking in the House, he adds to the argument from reason the argument from necessity.

"You may make the change tedious; you may make it violent; you may—God in His mercy forbid!—you may make it bloody; but avert it you cannot. Agitations of the public mind, so deep and so long continued as we have witnessed, do not end in nothing. In peace or in convulsion, by the law or in spite of the law, through the Parliament or over the Parliament, Reform must be carried. Therefore be content to guide that movement which you cannot stop. Fling wide the gates to that force which will else enter through the breach. Then will it still be, as it has hitherto been, the peculiar glory of our Constitution that, though not exempt from decay which is wrought by the vicissitudes of fortune and the lapse of time in all the proudest works of human power and wisdom, it yet contains the means of self-reparation. Then will England add to her manifold titles of glory this the noblest and purest of all; that every blessing which other nations have been forced to seek, and have too often sought in vain, by means of violent and bloody revolutions, she will have attained by a peaceful and a lawful Reform."

TWO

THE WHIG REFORMERS

THE HOUSE OF COMMONS which was elected in the new constituencies by the newly registered and qualified electors in 1832 was not startlingly different in its social composition from former House of Commons. No new class or type of Member came in in significant numbers; indeed there were only three English nonconformists in the new chamber. But it was radically different in one respect: the Tory party which had dominated the House for several decades and which had only just lost its majority in the elections of 1830 and 1831, was now very much weaker. In those days every Member had not a clear party label attached to him and estimates of party strength differed, but the figure generally agreed upon for the Tories was about 150. Not until 1906 did they sink to this figure again and even in 1945, which was reckoned to be a staggering defeat, their total was 213. The Parliament therefore was a Whig Parliament, a Parliament of Liberal tendencies.

In some respects the election had not been so much a contest of Whigs against Tories as of moderates against radicals. And in this contest the moderate candidates were on the whole very successful; the genuine radicals were few in number and of such varying views that they were not likely to stick closely together. But they were to be a stimulant to the reforming majority and their influence was to be out of proportion to their numbers. It must not be thought that they were men of vastly different antecedents from their fellows. If William Cobbett, elected to this Parliament, could be claimed as "a man of the people", Thomas Attwood, an unorthodox economist who was powerful in

Birmingham and was later to patronise the Chartists, was the son of a banker. Others who were called loosely "Bentha-mites" were such as Sir William Molesworth, eighth baronet of his line who had challenged his tutor at Cambridge to a duel, a sufficiently aristocratic attitude; Roebuck, Canadian born was a barrister and later a Q.C. The grandson of a famous inventor and industrialist, Grote, the historian, was a banker, Buller who was to be influential in colonial matters, was a barrister educated at Cambridge. Joseph Hume, the Scottish Radical economist, was originally a surgeon. Of these men it can be said that it was their minds and not their manners that made them different. They preached the radical philosophy which employed the idea of utility as a solvent to established institutions, they were believers in the individual's right to pursue his own happiness and could say with Bentham that they had learned to call the cause of the people the cause of virtue. They were inclined in return to call on the people to recognise philosophical radicalism as the path of wisdom.

The Government, the Ministry or, as it was often then called, the Administration, was not altered by the election nor was there any reason why it should be. The modern notion that at an election the people are called upon to "choose a government" was not then regarded as a necessary corollary of the constitution. Nor, if we reflect on it, is it now. The electors choose Members of the House of Commons to represent them; the Sovereign must find a Minister who can form an Administration which shall receive habitual support from the Commons and vote supplies and pass necessary legislation. It is only the strict organisation of modern parties that makes it seem as though electors chose the Government. The House of Commons is free to unmake it and in this century it has done so by insisting on party coalitions under pressure of war and in 1924 by unseating a Government which after an election had lost its majority while remaining the largest single party. Lord Grey and his colleagues therefore remained in office in perfect security. Their majority was immense even if it was unruly and liable to radical revolts on the left. And the ministry of Lord Grey was splendidly aristocratic. He himself was a great landowner, as were most of his colleagues. Lord Palmerston, the Foreign Secretary, owned land in England and Ireland, the Home Secretary, Lord Melbourne, was a landed magnate. The Chancellor of the Exchequer and leader of the Commons, Lord Althorp, was the son of an Earl, Sir James Graham, the First Lord of the Admiralty, was a rich Cumberland Baronet, Lord Durham was a man of extreme wealth but had the nickname of Radical Jack and was one of the principal authors of the Reform Bill. Lord John Russell was a Duke's son, the wealthiest of England's Dukes. The Lord Chancellor, Brougham, was a famous advocate who had made his name at the bar and in the House long since and was of less patrician though far from plebeian origins, Cockburn, the Lord Advocate for Scotland, was an eminent lawyer and one of the circle of the famous Edinburgh Review. Poulett-Thomson, the President of the Board of Trade, was conspicuously middle class, a merchant by profession. Of the actual Members of the Cabinet only four served in the House of Commons and of these two, Lord Althorp and Lord Palmerston were of the nobility, one the son of an Earl, the other an Irish Peer and so entitled to stand for election.

This pattern is often to be repeated. Peers and men of rank and wealth were to be given what seemed undue influence, and a large share of offices. For this there were three reasons, social, political and constitutional. As English society then stood men of wealth and rank were a necessary element to support the party in wealth and in prestige. As from 1835 to 1868 there was never a secure majority of more than a hundred in the Commons the party had to contain its more conservative elements and deal with radical revolts as they came. Constitutionally it had to have good representation in the House of Lords, where it was never in a majority and some of the great offices were traditionally held by Peers alone, such as Lord President of the Council and Lord Privy Seal.

There is one further observation about the party and its leaders. Parties tend to wax and wane not by any very great shifts of opinion amongst the electors. The electorate of this country for most of the time is and remains remarkably constant, not to say obstinate, in its political allegiances. If at times there are very large majorities in Parliament that is because the system of election by a simple relative majority vote provides that a small majority in votes cast in the country will be magnified in political representation in Parliament. Parties rise and fall more frequently by secessions and accretions. From the beginning of the Reform Bill crisis in 1830 up to 1833 the Whig-Liberal party benefited from a movement of this kind. The Tories were deeply divided; the Canningite section, liberal on the Catholic question, went over to Lord Grey. The remainder divided into those who accepted Wellington's betrayal on the Catholic emancipation Bill and those who did not cease to resent it. The Whigs embraced the Canningite seceders and accepted the support of the heterogeneous mass of Liberal and radical enthusiasts. But with the Reform question settled, the crisis over, there was less reason to rally to them. From that time onwards for more than two decades the party remained very static in its composition. In the eighteen forties the radical wing took a more definite form under the leadership of Cobden and Bright and what came to be called the Manchester school of economics and politics. In that decade the Tory party suffered from an irremediable split between the Peelites, who accepted free trade, and the orthodox rank and file Tories. By 1859 these Peelite elements, not numerous, but very able, serious and gifted, cohered with the Palmerstonian Whigs who threw out an arm also to the radicals and there came into existence the Liberal party proper. It was made more in Westminster than in the country. Then there would follow a long period of Liberal ascendancy. It did follow, with the one intermission of Disraeli's long ministry from 1874 to 1880. And then in 1886 the Liberals suffered from a devastating secession when Gladstone opted for Home Rule for Ireland. And now for twenty years the Liberals were out, except for one short interval between 1892 and 1895. In 1906 they returned with a triumphant victory. But was this entirely a movement of the spirit amongst the British people? By no means. The Conservatives, Unionists they now usually styled themselves, had committed the fatal error of schism and by allowing a section of the party to plunge them towards the still hated doctrine of protection lost many supporters, some into apathy and neutrality, some into active secession and opposition; of these the one name now remembered is that of young Winston Churchill. And even in the hour of their triumph the Liberals could see the writing on the wall, a new party called Labour, devoted to the needs and demands of "the workers", a party based on the support of the Trades Unions and inculcated with the doctrines of socialism; the party, to use an ugly foreign word, which has never had more than a pseudo-scientific and derisive vogue, of the proletariat.

When therefore we trace the evolution of the Liberal Party we must note what it stood for at any one time, what its philosophy was, what measures it promoted or fought against. But we must not think of these various "issues" as winners or losers amongst the people at large to any catastrophic degree. The allegiance of voters to a party is determined by many interests and sentiments of class-feeling and material inducement, religious attachment and also pure political interest and feeling. When a sufficient number of groups cohere to form a dominant and victorious party, then will the doctrine and policy of the party be most clearly demonstrated. In Liberal history we may denote three such epochs. The first was the years from 1830; the second was the era from 1868 dominated by Gladstone and the third the period from 1906 dominated by Lloyd George. It is the first period that we will now examine. Unlike the two later periods the period of efflorescence in the thirties has no dominant name, certainly not Grey or Melbourne, not Lord John Russell who was too limited and wayward, Brougham too eccentric. Bentham was dead, John Stuart Mill not yet mature. And in any case the radicals were an influence on the party rather than an element of the party. This period illustrates Liberal policy in government as an effort in reform under the impulsion of critical thought, criticism limited by custom and interest, by natural apathy and by the exhaustion of the public mind. When in 1841 the Whigs were defeated and gave place to the powerful Sir Robert Peel, Sydney Smith wrote that people felt that there was too much "botheration" about the Whigs. The country was tired of it. What was this? What were they bothering themselves and others about? What did they accomplish, what did they attempt and what did they ignore?

To answer these questions it is necessary to extract them from the continuum of history. There is no way out of this if we are to examine the elements that make up Liberal policy. But it must always be remembered that history consists of a series of confused events occurring simultaneously and our minds are jolted about from one thing to another; some things which we find to be important we scarcely notice at the time, others excite and exhaust us at the time and later we may forget about them or wonder why they caused us so much anxiety. It is always so. To understand history there is need for the continuous narrative method. For the period we are thinking about there is the third volume of Halévy's *History of the English People* which describes with wonderful penetration the confused events and issues of the eighteen thirties; there is Spencer Walpole's *History of England 1815–1856* which tells the story chronologically as seen by someone whose father was a mid-victorian statesman. There are many shorter histories which cover this period from which a knowledge of the sequence of events can be obtained.

In history one must think to some extent in parallel columns. For the student a good exercise is to construct your own table of events under broad headings.

With regard to government Liberals were always in something of a dilemma. The word Liberal means free and in the circumstances of the late eighteenth and early nineteenth century it meant primarily free from government restriction. In Europe before and during and after the Napoleonic wars nearly all governments were despotic, even the French Government under Napoleon which could be called popular but certainly not free. Only in a few countries such as Sweden did there linger the principle of control by Parliament or estates exercised over the Crown. Holland with its republican past had its own special form of freedom from despotic control. In the United States there was a federal republic solemnly dedicated to individual freedom and in it and in its constituent states there was indeed a community which enjoyed a freedom that no other peoples then knew. It was recognised to be very marvellous, whether horrifying or admirable. Persons of aristocratic mind feared and hated it; English radicals admired it; some even worshipped. The present phase in which the British Left show dislike and distrust of America is new and perhaps a passing phase. Americans were and are so conscious of their rebirth into freedom, which they date from the fourth of July 1776, that to the average American the notion that any other community can seriously claim to be their equals in freedom and in democracy is so ludicrous that they can scarcely admit it beyond the threshold of their minds. What has happened since 1830 is that slowly over large areas of Europe, with many interruptions and set-backs the western idea of liberal government has spread. In this movement the liberal practices of Great Britain under its ancient parliamentary system have been the most constant and on the whole the most effective factor whether acting as an agent or an example.

If Liberalism means to be free of government, this may

have two meanings. In its purest and most extreme sense it could mean as free as possible from all forms of government control. And this it did mean to many. In America, Thomas Jefferson who was both a great statesman and a philosopher had said that that government governs best which governs least. Many in England thought the same. Utilitarian thought, centred on the needs of the individual, was, with some exceptions and abatements, adverse to meddling by government or at least by governments as they had been. Later in the century a somewhat crude application of Darwin's concept of the survival of the fittest to political affairs led to the belief that the individual should have the fullest freedom to find his level and improve his lot. Herbert Spencer (1820 to 1903) was to be the great exponent of Man versus the State which he made the title of a book. After outlining the limits within which a man must be restrained from interfering with others, he concludes, "There is maintained the vital principle of social progress; inasmuch as, under such conditions, the individuals of most worth will prosper and multiply more than those of less worth." And he states with something like prophetic insight, "It would need but a war with an adjacent society, or some internal discontent demanding forcible suppression, to at once transform a socialistic administration into a grinding tyranny like that of ancient Peru; under which the mass of the people controlled by grades of officials, and leading lives that were inspected out-of-doors and indoors, laboured for the support of the organisation which regulated them, and were left with but a bare subsistence for themselves." But it was not as simple as this. Liberal reformers distrusted the state as they knew it. But they were often zealots for "improvement" and men often have a strange reluctance to being improved. Note that in the first half of the century "improvement" was the usual word; later the word "progress" came to replace it but improvement is the better, for it suggests some effort and agency and is not associated with the idea of natural and inevitable progress which became so common until the black storms of the twentieth century put it under a cloud. The Liberal view may be described as follows. All exercise of power by the state must be carefully scrutinised before permitted: the general presumption was against it. But many would hold that the right kind of state, the wisely directed government under due representative control, might well do more in some fields than it had been used to do.

On one thing all were agreed. Despotic governments, governments in which the sovereign, be he a monarch or a self-perpetuating oligarchy, could rule without criticism and restraint by the public, such governments were bad. And be it remembered that in the first half of the century by far the greater part of Europe was under such despotic government. This was not the danger in Great Britain. By the Revolution of 1688 mere monarchial despotism had been exorcised. It was thought that later some of it had crept back under George III in the guise of a controlled oligarchy. This oligarchy had been smitten hard by the great Reform Bill but more remained to be done. The rational Whig-Liberals set about this.

One big change was made in 1835. The suffocating gothic diversity and quite unrepresentative organisation of the towns of England was regularised and reformed and the regularisation was not the least part of the reform. After enquiry by the now very favourite device of a Royal Commission the Municipal Corporations Act provided for a uniform scheme for all boroughs in England and Wales, 187 in number, and an equivalent act was passed for Scotland. There were to be annual elections of one third of the council, public audit of accounts; the control was to be in the hands of the rate-payers, who should have the right to vote and whose interest was to see good and economic administration. Here we see satisfied the two criteria of regularity, all to be the same, and responsibility, the people who paid the taxes to control the election to the council. It took a Liberal Government to do this; the Tories could not have accomplished such a sweeping and complete reform. In all essentials this scheme is with us still, so far as the organisation of town councils is concerned, although the franchise is now universal. Perhaps it is now too much of a strait-jacket and prevents municipal life from experimenting and inventing. But it was a bold measure and very complete. It did not however touch the administration of the counties to the chagrin of the hard-thinking radicals. But the Whigs knew the law of their own preservation; they knew that England was a deeply traditional country and that the landed families, the men of property and men of ancestry, were still in so many ways the effective leaders of the community: one could not try them too hard.

Another great institutional change was made in the organisation of the Poor Law. Here we must distinguish between the institutions set up to work the Poor Law and the treatment given to the destitute which is a difficult and different story. Once again we see the same factors at work, regularisation and responsibility. The Poor Law Amendment Act of 1834 laid down that the parishes, small, irregular and uneconomic units for the purpose, should be united into new areas of government called Poor Law Unions. This was for England and Wales: in Scotland until 1845 poor relief was still a function of the Kirk. The new unions of parishes were to cross even county boundaries if geography and sense dictated it. The unions were to be controlled by elected Boards of Guardians on a franchise of rate-payers. With an oligarchic quirk the wealthier payers of rates were to be given more votes. These unions and guardians lasted in effect until 1929. It is worth dwelling on this wholesale marking out of areas over the country for a specific governmental purpose: it had never happened since the shires had slowly come into existence in the mists of Saxon antiquity.

But it was not enough to say that the new authorities must

be delineated and set going. It could not be done without central control and the appointment of many paid officials. The Whig Government faced this and appointed commissioners for the Poor Law who sat in Somerset House in London and under them many officers to visit the shires and establish the new areas and machinery. Soon a storm was beating on them. Those who looked for less government from Liberals were hostile; moreover the Whigs had made great play with the great number of government posts in the hands of the Ministry and here they were creating more, more expense, more patronage. Much as the Tory gentry welcomed the promised relief from Poor Rates that the Act foreshadowed they could not fail to rub in the moral. English gentlemen felt that they should run their own counties and parishes and not be interfered with by jacks-in-office and government mischiefmakers. The matter is satirised by Peacock in *Crotchet Castle* in which he describes a gentlemanly parson being quizzed by some charity commissioners. "And what in the name of all that is wonderful can those fellows mean? They have come here in a chaise and four to make a fuss about a pound per annum which after all they leave as it was. I wonder who pays them for their trouble and how much?" It was all part of the "botheration" admitted by Sydney Smith. But the botheration went on and the archbotherer was Edwin Chadwick, the indefatigable secretary of the Poor Law Commission. Eventually the storm was too great and he had to go (1846), but not until the structure of the new poor law organisation was erected.

This problem was to remain with the Liberals and indeed all successive English governments. The Liberals, and still more their radical allies, held the view that before their advent to power there was very much that was amiss in English government. There had been an "ancien régime", that of "the Tory oligarchy". But if we consider the nature of English eighteenth century government we will find that what we would mostly agree to be its defects were of different kinds. To some extent it was a misgoverned country, too much royal influence, too much oligarchical power, too little public control of the Government. But it suffered in many ways from being an ungoverned country; the freedom of highwaymen and robbers was notorious and shocking to citizens of the stronger governments of the Continent; the terrible Gordon riots of 1780 had startled Europe. The government of England had to be made more free and popular, it had to be made more economical and it had to be made more efficient. All these aims could not be pursued without conflict between them. Thus popular commotions caused by the new poor law, strikes or later chartist agitation, could only be suppressed by the heavy hand of the army. Sir Robert Peel had created the Metropolitan Police in 1829 and it was not a moment too soon. These "janissaries", "praetorian guards", (many horrid foreign names were devised for them), were at first not popular. The Whig ministry kept them in being but were lax, there were those who said cowardly, in failing properly to support them. But by the end of the decade in many parts the situation was serious. In 1839 an act was passed to set up police forces in each county. The Home Secretary as the agent of the central government could prescribe uniform regulations for the police over the whole country; but the local control was left with the justices of the peace for the county. The principle of central control was exercised to the minimum. Liberalism had to make its terms with oligarchy.

Not only in police work does government require agents. The average Whig reformer before coming to power expressed himself with genuine indignation against the numbers of functionaries appointed and paid by the Government. To these the general name of "placemen" was given. Some offices were mere sinecures, offices with salary but no serious work attached. Burke had struck the first blow at this system in 1782, but there were still many offices to be given and a considerable number of pensions. These abuses were to go. "We are to lose our pension", wrote the Tory Mrs. Arbuthnot in her diary in 1831 when her husband's pension given by George IV was in danger. And the movement to abolish sinecure offices and political pensions continued. But the task of reform had to go on. You cannot sweep a stable without a broom. The Poor Law, the Factory Acts, the numerous investigations into charities suspected of being abusively used, led to many appointments. Often enough the choice was wise and good hard-working officials were given the task. But it cannot be too often remembered that at this time the appointment of government servants was in the hands of the ministers of the Crown and their deputies. The idea of a civil service as a profession distinct from others and regulated by severe competitive rules was then unknown. As we shall see it was established in the third quarter of the century, but until it was, all appointments were open to the suspicion of political, personal and family favour. And the Whig ministers were very human men; they had families, friends, dependents and clients, lean kine who had known the years of dearth. Were they not to be brought to the rich pastures now?

Many of the characteristics of modern England which we are apt to regard as being inherent in the national character are in fact the work of government over the long years. Englishmen pride themselves on their orderliness, their readiness to abstain from violence and to support order. But this is not by any means a gift of nature; it is a work of art. The modern Englishman, admiring his famous police force, aiding and co-operating with them, is what he is very much by means of these police and he need only to look back on his violent and riotous past to see the difference. The modern Englishman too is proud of the freedom from corruption which is the boast of our press and public. He is genuinely horrified by tales of the "corruption", the giving of offices by political, religious or family favour, which he hears of in the eastern and western hemispheres. But this has arisen from our practice of insulating the public service from these forms of influence and favour.

A distinguished diplomatist, the late Sir David Kelly, has said in his book *The Ruling Few* that Englishmen persistently fail to understand that in many societies, the near-east and southern and Catholic Europe, morality places the claims of the family against the state far higher than is known here. He adds that he can discern a difference here between the English and the Irish and the Scots who show a stronger sense of the claims of kindred.

The growth of the independent civil service idea was contributed to by many political elements. It was never a pure party matter. But the greatest impulse and the most fruitful preparation for it came from Liberal-intellectual circles and the most important leader in the movement was a Liberal statesman, Charles Trevelyan, the brother-in-law of the Whig Macaulay. It is he who is amusingly satirised by Anthony Trollope as Sir Gregory Hardlines in his civil service novel, *The Three Clerks*.

The decade of the eighteen thirties was not only a crucial age in political development, it was also a time of great religious interest. The first rush of reforming zeal seemed to threaten not only the old régime in the state but in the church as well. The Whig ministers were lax and laodicean in their attitude to the church, although they recognised its existence as a political necessity. But on either side of them were powerful forces which they might disdain as fanatics but which were not to be ignored. The Protestant dissenters, and still more their radical secularist allies, looked to a time when the monopoly of the established church would be abolished; they saw in the United States a country in which full religious freedom existed and much religious fervour without a single remnant of the idea of legal establishment. Their resentment was deep and bitter and perhaps very narrow, only to be equalled by the contemptuous hiss with which an Anglican parson could pronounce the word

Dissent. John Bright was later to sum up what he thought were the pretensions of the Church in these words. "It always seems to me to come from that appetite for supremacy which springs from the fact that we have in this country a powerful and dominant Church, connected chiefly with a powerful ruling class, and that step by step the people of this country, one section after another, have wrested from that Church and from that class, the rights of citizenship which we have claimed and which we now enjoy."

In the first flush of reform it is not surprising that the Dissenters might hope to realise their aims. But a counter offensive was on its way. A group of young Oxford dons, clerics of course, began from 1833 onwards that movement which was at first Tractarian and later the Oxford movement and is now known by the name of Anglo-Catholic. Keble, Newman and Pusey and the leaders of this movement found a large audience in their *Tracts for the Times* and personally in their preaching in Oxford. They spoke of the Church of England as part of the Church universal, truly catholic, with rights and duties that the state could in no wise abrogate and which it must, if it be a Christian state, support. Their influence was profound on the few serious "reading men" of Oxford, perhaps not more than five hundred at a time. Amongst these was William Ewart Gladstone of Christ Church soon to be a Tory Member of Parliament and he was to write his first book in 1838 on the State in its relations with the Church. He had no thought of separation and he wrote in a lyrical strain, "Her foundations are upon the Holy hills."

Holy hills or no, the Whig ministers understood that something must be done about the Church. Disregarding the wild Catholic reactionaries of Oxford, they leaned more on the latitudinarians, the broad churchmen or, within reason, on the protestant evangelical section of the church. They promoted broad churchmen of abilities and attacked the Irish Church Establishment by uniting dioceses and appro-

priating revenues saved for church building and clergy
stipends. Church rates in Ireland were ended. But even this
cost them the resignation of three ministers, Lord Stanley,
Sir James Graham, the Duke of Richmond. When they came
to deal with the Church of England they were careful. They
did not go so far that they could not count on the general
support of Peel. Several acts reorganised the dioceses, cut
down the large incomes and made a fund to aid the poorer
clergy. Pluralism, the holding of several benefices together,
was forbidden except in exceptional cases. Marriage elsewhere than in Anglican Churches was permitted. The
rationalising spirit was given some play. Liberalism reached
a working rule about established churches. Where obviously
a large majority of the people were hostile to the established
church the establishment had to go, as in Ireland in 1869 and
in Wales in 1914. In England and Scotland an impasse was
reached and is still in existence. The purest Liberal theory
is averse to monopoly, control or preference by the state in
things religious. But where an established church is in being
and is reasonably representative, maintaining the cherished
and traditional forms of the national religion, Liberals do
not move to upset it. The old bitternesses are mellowing;
we are all Whigs now. The Queen is crowned by the Archbishop surrounded by Prelates in full pomp and panoply, the
Moderator of the Church of Scotland presents her with a
Bible, "These are the lively oracles of God." How strange it
would seem to the militant Dissenters and the disdainful
secularists of the eighteen thirties, twelve decades after the
year of the Great Reform. And here we must notice that the
Liberal Party, while harbouring always strong anti-clerical
elements, never became an anti-religious party. Here it was
very different from parties on the Left on the Continent,
where the clash between clerical and anti-clerical became so
bitter and usually represented a difference between a
Catholic and an atheist. In countries like Spain, Portugal,
Italy and France, to be a Liberal meant not merely a critic

or enemy of a particular form of religious establishment; it meant an enemy of religion or at least a person quite indifferent to its claims. When Pope Pius IX in his famous encyclical declared, "*Liberalismus anathema sit*", he might be thinking of Garibaldi; he was not thinking of Gladstone.

The Whig-Liberals of this period were often denounced by their enemies, Tory or radical, as being rather dry and rational pedants, indifferent to the things of the spirit, obsessed with blue books and royal commissions, men of little feeling, to use a phrase still very far in the future "dessicated calculating machines". Disraeli was hitting at this when he makes a character in his famous political novel, *Coningsby*, say that "even Mormon counts more votaries than Bentham". But men like Grey and Althorp, Durham and Russell, the eldest of whom had heard the glowing eloquence and known the inexpressible charm of the great Charles Fox, these men would claim to be men not only of reason but of heart. Was there nothing in their schemes to alleviate the ills of some part of suffering humanity? There was. It had been the work of Fox in his last brief spell of office to carry through an act for the ending of the slave trade in African negroes. True he was not the only or indeed the chief advocate of this measure. That distinction goes to the Tory Evangelical Wilberforce, the close friend of the younger Pitt. But the heirs of Fox favoured the extension of the reform of slavery and Wilberforce was still living until 1833, keeping up his crusade for nothing less than the abolition of slavery under the British Crown, which meant in effect in the West Indian Islands. The Government decided to fulfil in a radical manner the demands of the evangelical zealots, many of them Tories. Stanley, who had become Colonial Secretary, rapidly prepared a Bill; he had as his principal secretary the well-known colonial expert James Stephen, a keen evangelical himself. Through a long Sunday, working for the first and last time on the sabbath, Stephen completed the Bill which was eventually carried after long debates. Slavery came to an end on 1st August 1834 and the sum of £20,000,000 was paid in compensation to owners. Troubles were to follow in Jamaica and elsewhere as the owners of plantations ran into difficulties over the period of indenture that the labourers had to serve before their final freedom, and discipline was hard to maintain. But meanwhile Parliament had to turn to another humanitarian problem at home; while public money was being lavished on the slaves of Jamaica there were those who heard the cry of "the slaves of Yorkshire". The employment of women and children in factories had engaged the attention of philanthropic people for some time past. The father of Sir Robert Peel, himself a mill owner, had promoted the first factory act in 1802. Now the demand was stronger and voiced by such men as the Tory M.P. and mill-owner, Oastler and a young nobleman, Lord Ashley, afterwards Lord Shaftesbury. Here again was the conflict between the principle of freedom from the state and the need for government control to protect the weak. All through the century it was to perplex Liberals and in 1895 the famous Liberal statesman John Morley, the biographer of Cobden, was to lose his seat at Newcastle partly because he would not accept the project of an eight hour day for miners. There were two questions, the right of Parliament to legislate for children and limit their labour even when the parents were willing to sell it. This was generally conceded to be right in principle. Lord Althorp furthered a Bill originally proposed by Ashley which limited the hours of older children and prohibited factory labour for children under nine. It applied only to certain types of mill. To make sure of some enforcement inspectors were appointed to visit the factories. More power to salaried officials.

The second question was whether the labour of adults should be limited by law. This was mooted in the thirties but the great struggle was to arise in the forties and to be settled by an act of 1847. It was never a pure party matter. Both parties had supporters of factory Bills and both had enemies.

However the manufacturers as a class had an interest against such legislation and the smaller and economically weaker especially feared ruin from a sudden cutting off of their supply of labour. The country gentry who had their own standards of charity to the poor were genuinely shocked by factory conditions and had little sympathy with the mill owners, their political enemies who seemed to be ruining the face of England with their ugly mills. The manufacturers, living so much in small, new, industrial towns, self-made men, suspicious and resentful of the gentry, men to whom a squire was in the nature of things a tyrant, regarded with astonished resentment these sermons from the age-long oppressors of the poor, who indeed were willing to pocket complacently enough the rents of the land which the manufacturers and their workers had covered with factories, houses and shops. Not until the Marxian challenge to all property, land or capital, united all the possessing classes did this sore spot in English life cease to rankle.

THREE

THE GOSPEL OF FREE TRADE

WE HAVE so far left out of our account of Liberal thought and action one element which is often thought to be its most important and characteristic, its theory of wealth and production. We live in an age in which it is customary for any persons or interests who feel their livelihood endangered to request, require and, if they have the power, to command that "the Government" must do something about it, must come to their aid with schemes and subsidies or save them from ruin by excluding the products of other lands and controlling the immigration of strangers who will take the bread out of our mouths. An industry feels itself to be in peril, be it agriculture, cotton, coal-mining or ship-building. Members of Parliament must be moved to ask questions, candidates at elections must be grilled with demands for promises of support, the Government, the Government, always the Government, must act. Now this idea, to which we are all accustomed, is probably the more normal experience of most communities in human history. Sovereigns, princes, magistrates, guilds and other bodies with established power have usually conceived that the regulation of trade in great matters and in small was part of their duty; the wealth of the community has usually seemed to be the concern of the rulers. It seemed natural that it should be. The period we are dealing with here is an exceptional period in history, an age in which in many countries, but most of all in Scotland and England, and the United States, the belief grew that the wealth of the community was not the product of wise governmental direction but on the contrary flourished most when that direction was least.

The first shot in this long campaign for economic liberty was fired in the year 1776, the year of the American Revolution. It was fired by a Professor of Moral Philosophy in Glasgow University, Adam Smith, in his *Inquiry into the Nature and Causes of the Wealth of Nations*. Swiftly it became famous and in due course it became a canon of economic wisdom. The Foxite Whigs were negligent of its lessons and for a time left the field to Pitt. But by the coming of peace in 1815 and still more by the time of the Reform Bill the rising generation of Liberal thinkers and above all the bankers, traders and manufacturers who formed such a large section of the party, were treating it as a fount of wisdom. The main theme of the book, which abounds in historical examples and information on the economies of many nations, was that the production of wealth thrives best when left to the enterprise of producers on the principle of a natural liberty. In a famous passage the author states:

"As every individual, therefore, endeavours as much as he can both to employ his capital in the support of domestic industry and so to direct that industry that its produce may be of the greatest value, every individual necessarily labours to render the annual revenue of the society as great as he can. He generally indeed, neither intends to promote the public interest nor knows how much he is promoting it. By preferring the support of domestic industry to that of foreign industry, he intends only his own security; and by directing that industry in such a manner as its produce may be of the greatest value, he intends only his own gain, and he is in this, as in many other cases, led by an invisible hand to promote an end which was no part of his intention. Nor is it always the worse for the society that it was no part of it. By pursuing his own interest he frequently promotes that of the society more effectually than when he really intends to promote it. I have never known much good done by those who affected to trade for the public good. It is an affectation indeed not very common among merchants, and very few

words need be employed in dissuading them from it."
(*Wealth of Nations*, Book IV, chapter ii.)

In an earlier paper Adam Smith in 1755 had expressed the
same idea more simply. "Little else is requisite to carry a
state to the highest degree of opulence from the lowest
barbarism, but peace, easy taxes and a tolerable administration of justice; all the rest being brought out by the natural
order of things. All governments which thwart this natural
course, which force things into another channel or which
endeavour to arrest the progress of society at a particular
point are unnatural, and to support themselves are obliged
to be oppressive and tyrannical." (Quoted by Dugald Stuart,
Introduction to *The Wealth of Nations*, Routledge 1895).

Bentham in 1798, extending his individualist philosophy
into the field of economics, had come to the same conclusion.
"The general rule is that nothing ought to be done or
attempted by government. The motto or watchword of
government, on these occasions, ought to be—Be quiet."

Now if this was true, the consequences were profound. The
field of government in economic life must be severely res-
tricted. Restrictions on trade and manufacture, restrictions
on the use of labour, import duties and prohibitions all must
go or only be maintained in the case of extreme necessity.
And if it was all true, the individual working to increase his
own wealth would appear as a public benefactor, a valuable
agent in the prosperity of his country. Before 1830 there had
been some important steps towards the freeing of trade by
Huskisson, the Canningite President of the Board of Trade.
But there were still tariffs on most imports and navigation
was not fully free to foreign ships. It might be thought that
with such a general ascendancy amongst writers and thinkers
and with the natural support of the business community, the
evolution to free trade might have been easy. Such however
was not the expectation of Adam Smith in his own time.
In *The Wealth of Nations* (Book IV, chapter ii) he remarks:
"To expect indeed that the freedom of trade should ever be

entirely restored in Great Britain is as absurd as to expect that Oceania or Utopia should ever be established in it. Not only the prejudices of the public but what is more unconquerable, the private interests of many individuals, irresistibly oppose it." And yet it was done. By the third quarter of the nineteenth century no tariffs were left except a few tolerated only for the convenience of revenue and these were light. This work was the work of the new Liberal Party. It was so much their work and so much their doctrine that they were accused at times of being incapable of thinking of any other public object. But this was not true.

The battle for freedom of trade was mixed up with political passions and class antipathies. There is nothing rarer in history than a pure economic motive in politics. Even when it seems to be supreme, other elements enter in. No man likes to stand before others merely as an advocate of his own gain. He desires to import some other value, social, political or even religious. There was one particular issue which became the centre of the struggle, the corn laws. This was like a bastion which, if it fell, would lead to the complete surrender of the fortress and on both sides this was understood. The corn laws, duties on imported cereals, principally wheat, were the best point for free trade attack. For one thing it was a fairly new impost. Until after the middle of the eighteenth century England could usually supply its own corn. Later it found it hard to grow enough to support its rising population. Import of foreign corn was forbidden if the price at home was below a certain figure; if the price rose then a duty was charged on a sliding scale which fell as corn grew dearer. This form of protection was justified by protectionists on the grounds that it was necessary to protect what was after all by far the largest single industry. But agriculture was to be protected because it was more than an industry, it was a way of life. It was the primal human activity, nourished by the sweat of Adam. It represented Old England, the secure, sane, traditional ways of English life, the squire, the parson, the farmer and his men, whom if you wanted to be poetic you called husbandmen. This way of life was threatened by the new men, the men who set up mills and mines, whose chimneys were fouling the air, whose works were defiling the rivers and who drew together in wretched hovels a new mis-shapen race of men and women, wretched and helpless and a prey to cheap demagogues, careless of their duty to God and King and Church.

On the other hand the Liberal industrialists and merchants and many of their workers saw in the attempt to keep the price of bread a singularly insolent attempt of the possessing few, of the too long established oligarchs, to maintain their social and political supremacy against the clear dictates of reason and to the detriment, perhaps the ruin, of the rising, active, intelligent, wealth-creating and not wealth-consuming classes. If you could make a myth of agriculture you could make a myth of bread, the staff of life, the only substance mentioned in the Lord's Prayer. Bread for the people, cheap bread, good bread, was there ever a simpler and more impressive election cry? Even in 1910 the cry was in full swing and the hoardings all over Britain were covered with Liberal posters showing the small nasty dark loaf eaten by the "protected" foreigner and the large, fine white loaves of the free trade British.[1] Agitation against the "iniquitous" corn laws never ceased from the time they were imposed but did not become a major matter of dispute until the close of the thirties when the agitation was firmly organised with its centre in Manchester. In October 1838 Richard Cobden, a young manufacturer who had emigrated from the South and made Lancashire his home, and in time his spiritual kingdom, joined a group of Manchester men in an anti-corn law

---

[1] Speaker Lowther, a member of a fine old Tory family, when he summoned the victorious Liberal Ministers in 1910 to the customary dinner, instructed his butler to serve to each a brown and a white roll and observed with glee that the Free Trade statesmen one by one crumbled the brown and rejected the white.

committee which was soon to be federated with many similar bodies to form the Anti-Corn Law League. He roused his friend John Bright of Rochdale from mourning the young wife he had just lost and they set out on a crusade for their supreme aim, the total abolition of duties on corn.

The story of this strange social and political war can be followed in the pages of John Morley's *Life of Cobden*, the work of an ardent disciple. In the luminous and judicious writing of Sir John Clapham's *Economic History of England* a more eclectic and balanced view can be obtained. Lives of Peel by Parker, Miss Ramsay and others show how the bombardment by the particles of Cobden's relentless arguments slowly moved that fine, firm, but not immovable intellect to a final conversion. In Moneypenny's *Disraeli* we can read of the bitter but unavailing revenge of the betrayed Tories. The struggle was waged on paper and in speech, in Parliament and in urban streets and even carried into remote rural villages. Each side believed not only in the right but the righteousness of its cause. The defenders foreboded a surrender of the country to the town, of the natural leaders of he nation to a new and rootless race of huckstering bagmen, a grim exercise in the materialistic calculus, a shameless repetition of the word, "cheap", buy in the cheapest market, sell in the dearest and the devil take the hindmost. The Free Traders saw the defeat of a narrow and insolent aristocracy, the unlimited improvement of the national wealth, the liberation of the labouring poor from the dreadful fluctuation in the price of their chief, perhaps their only food. They saw too with visionary zeal a picture of the nations of the civilised world rallying to the new gospel and recognising the interdependence of each on all, renouncing the horrible arbitrament of war, casting away the armaments that weighed so hard on the peoples and with them the pride and arrogance of the military caste with its terrible appetite for supremacy at home and abroad, its love of glory and of blood.

While this dispute went on, in the broadest terms a dispute

between the country and the town, the north and the south, the middle class and the aristocracy, another turmoil was going on; the agitation of the chartists. They were a part, no more, of the working classes in the towns, radical and republican, fiercely democratic, demanding not only the ballot but manhood suffrage and annual parliaments. They refused to be led by Cobden and his friends; they scented hypocrisy in the fine phrases about ameliorating the lot of the poor; they suspected that cheap bread really meant lower wages. But Cobden outgeneralled them all; he had the staff, the men of education and sufficient means, the whole power of the reputable economists of the day, the possession of an organisation ably directed to one simple and self-satisfying end, the repeal of the taxes on corn. The Chartists were defeated; their last throw in 1848, two years after the repeal was in the end a farce. They disbanded; as a force they were no more. But they continued as a leaven and although few there were always working men who felt that Cobden had cheated them of their great chance by his fiscal magic, his part as a pied piper who had called the simple workers after him when they might have struck a blow for the people, carried out a really glorious revolution of the people for the people. Some of the descendants of these men never rallied to the Liberal Party. They leaned to the various embryo forms of socialism and considered the bosses, the bourgeoisie, their prime enemy. In the twentieth century many socialists would hate the name of Cobden as much as any Tory.

The economy of the country grew and developed in a most remarkable fashion during the nineteenth century and most of this growth was not caused or even very much regulated by government. In some matters, as we have seen the Government had in the end to interfere; it controlled the employment of women and children in mines and factories and eventually limited the labour even of adults. As machines came more into use and became more dangerous, stricter factory laws had to be made as a precaution against accidents.

New forms of transport, such as the railways which came to cover the island in the forties and fifties, had to be regulated both for safety and also with maximum prices, for even while there were competing companies railway transport had something of the quality of a monopoly until in our own time it has been challenged by road and air. The Board of Trade had to regulate merchant shipping also for safety and for the protection of the crews. Parliament also could not be indifferent to the forms in which industry was organised and an elaborate branch of law grew up which is called company law: this provides rules for the formation and the working of the joint stock company, usually now a limited liability company, which is the characteristic form of industrial enterprise. This was necessary to protect the subscribers of shares in these companies from fraud and mismanagement. But in the mid-nineteenth century many, indeed most businesses, were family and personal and depended on the skill and industry of the owners and directors of the business, persons for whom by some linguistic freak it has never been found possible to find a good English name. Economists use the French word "entrepreneur".

As the wealth of the country grew steadily, as the factories and shipyards multiplied, as British goods were carried all over the world mainly by British ships, and all this without direction, favour or patronage of the state, it is not surprising that it came to be generally agreed that Adam Smith was right. Natural liberty was doing more for the material progress of the world than any other force. The men who bent the whole of their secular thoughts to this amazing task of material production did not feel that they had anyone to thank for it but themselves. This is particularly well illustrated in the life of Scotland which in this epoch grew from being a materially backward country to being a rich industrial country, until by the beginning of the twentieth century the river Clyde alone built more ships than any other area in the world and built them larger. The one political condition necessary for this was the freedom of trade with England and all the British dominions. It required no government action; there was no Secretary of State and no Scottish office. And the people of Scotland were in the main Liberals. How little they worried then about national independence or dictation from Whitehall may seem to us now rather strange. A recent writer, Mr. J. M. Reid, (*Scotland Past and Present*, Home University Library: pp. 34 and 41) has written:

"It is not surprising that a people who had liquidated their own national State should have been attracted by the thought that in economic affairs (and a good many others) the State should do as little as possible. During the century and more when government direction of trade and industry was dwindling Scottish business did, in fact, flourish dramatically." And again: "And all or almost all of this had been created by Scotsmen of the last few generations without the help or intervention of any political authority."

In recent times the doctrines of Adam Smith and his successors have been attacked from socialist and other sources as being a "gospel of greed." What force is there in this charge? It should be remembered that economics is not ethics and that Adam Smith was engaged in a purely economic theorem. He was trying to expound how a community could grow wealthier in all its parts. He was not concerned to say what were the misuses of wealth or any other form of power. As a Professor of Moral Philosophy he dealt with that in another part of the course. There are however certain moral and political dangers in telling men that the more they strive to enrich themselves the more they benefit the whole community. Let us remember his actual words.

"By pursuing his own interest he frequently promotes that of the society more effectually than when he really intends to promote it." There is a presumption that what he does for his own good he does for the benefit of all. If he is told that the public interest requires that he should be curbed and restrained in his economic activities he is not likely to consider calmly and objectively whether the claim of the public in this case be true. He will probably become indignant and, knowing that the argument of his own profit will impress no one, he will fall back on the general thesis that free enterprise is always best and its opponents always wrong. In this way most Liberal industrialists opposed factory regulation; they objected to interference on philanthropic grounds or on grounds of national defence, arguing that the decline of total wealth caused by these restraints would be a greater evil than the specific evils that the interference was calculated to prevent. Here is a temptation to dishonesty and arrogance.

But is it greater than in other cases? According to men's different social position and prejudices wealth is odious in differing degrees. To the secure and established elements in society there is always something very offensive about new and growing wealth. It is by its very existence a disturbance, an intrusion in the social system. The newly rich man is an alarming phenomenon. Once he was not; there he is; you knew him when he was going his rounds on a cart or working in the mill in his shirt-sleeves. And now he will speak to you as an equal, almost, it seems scarcely credible, patronise you. The Liberal party in the nineteenth century stripped of its top-dressing of Whig gentlemen was very much a party of the middle class industrialists, merchants and business men of all kinds. In the social hierarchy of the day they were subject to limitations, slights and what Hobbes has called "signs of undervalue." In response it was natural that they should take the counter-offensive and consider their form of wealth as socially valuable, to use a modern term, "functional", as opposed to the idle inherited wealth of the aristocracy, created and maintained by the work of others, paid in rent and interest. Why should profit be despised? Able and industrious men, courageous men, willing to risk, made profits; others did not. And so there was a grumbling class-war between the middle and the upper classes. Bright and Cobden fought it; later the young Joseph Chamberlain in his radical days pointed it sharply when he said of the landlords, "they toil not, neither do they spin."

And if newly made wealth is odious to the secure possessing landed classes it is also odious to the poorer workers, to those who have been left behind in the race, those who see their former mates advance to affluence, live in grander houses, reach the seats of dignity and power in the locality. Why did they succeed? There is always an element of luck in human life and the lack of it is the easiest recourse in argument of those who do not succeed. Why did one man become an entrepreneur, a capitalist, able to employ the labour of others instead of merely hiring his own? Was it natural ability, temperance, industry, thrift, insight, courage and determination? Or was it a small legacy, a prudent marriage, a smooth tongue to social superiors? And why was the poor man left behind? There might be many causes, thriftlessness, drunkenness, laziness, indiscipline and pugnacity, or perhaps ill-health in himself or his family, sheer misfortune in the accident of employment and unemployment, the need to keep a roof over a family of younger brothers and sisters. No one can pronounce with certainty on any of these things. But while all allowance is made for the accidents and vicissitudes of life, the people of that age very widely believed that success in worldly affairs was usually the result of some merit. Nor must it be supposed that the weekly wage earners did not often admire as well as envy the man who made his way up the ladder. There was a scale and hierarchy amongst the weekly wage earners as amongst the workers on their own account, some of whom might come to be capitalists and rich men. The urge to self-improvement was strong. Those who fared further were recognised as the rightful winners of the race. In 1860 Engels, Marx's disciple, complains sourly:

"It seems that this most bourgeois of all nations wants to bring matters to such a pass as to have a bourgeois aristocracy

and a bourgeois proletariat side by side with the bourgeoisie," Quoted, Popper, *The Open Society and Its Enemies*, II, p. 175.

The Liberal doctrine of free trade and absence of government control placed the Liberals in a position of great difficulty with regard to the working men when it came to Trades Unions. A free economy in its fullest sense means freedom to employ your labour as you please; this means for the employer freedom to make his terms with the individual worker and for the worker the freedom to make his terms with any employer. Now this pure and perfect freedom is an abstraction. It never fully exists. The worker seeking work cannot usually in practice have a very free choice of employment. For one thing he is settled in one place; he may move but, especially if he has a wife and family, it is not easy. Adam Smith noticed this when he observed that "man is of all forms of luggage the most difficult to be moved". The balance between master and man may occasionally tip on the side of the man but is more usually tipped on the side of the master. The weekly wage earner must earn weekly; he has nothing to fall back upon. Moreover he may have some special skill or aptitude which is easy to employ only in certain places and in certain times. A general decline of some industry may put him in a hopeless bargaining position. To recompense themselves for this natural disadvantage the workers have one supreme remedy, combination. They may combine to withdraw the labour of them all and for this purpose they need organisation to direct their moves and savings to make the withdrawal, as the strike is called, possible.

At the beginning of our period Trades Unions were bodies suspect to the political classes and with inadequate rights in law. In 1824 old laws against the combination of workers had been repealed and this produced so many strikes that next year Parliament modified the law and recognised Trades Unions but with severe limitations on their activities **and** permitting them only for the sole purpose of consulting upon and determining the rate of wages and prices. In the years after 1830 there was much unrest in the country including the country districts of the south later to become so quiet and submissive. Melbourne, who was Home Secretary and charged with the preservation of law and order, acted with great firmness towards these discontents and in 1834 he authorised an act which has become legendary, the deportation of the Tolpuddle martyrs. Tolpuddle is a small Dorset village from which six labourers were sentenced for "administering illegal oaths". Radical opinion was roused and there were loud protests. It seems that in this particular case the punishment was out of all proportion to the crime but it should be remembered that in the unpoliced counties of these days order was not easily kept. The Liberal industrialists as a class had a strong interest against trades union action. There was always a minority who took a more lenient view but we find Cobden saying that he had rather be under a Dey of Algiers than under the rule of a Trades Committee.

The early nineteenth century Liberal economists believed that wages were determined by conditions of supply and demand and held that the efforts of labourers by combinations to improve their lot flew in the face of economic facts. They hoped continually, but ineffectually, that the labourers would in due course recognise this truth. The most eminent of these economists, David Ricardo, held that Labour had its natural price, the price necessary to enable the labourers to subsist and its market price, the price which is actually paid from the natural operation of the proportion of the supply to the demand. If the market price is high then the labourers flourish but not otherwise. He concludes, "Like all other contracts, wages should be left to the fair and free competition of the market and should never be controlled by the influence of the legislature."

This doctrine, so comfortable to the employers, was never accepted by the labourers in this country. The growth of British industry has gone on side by side with the growth of

Trades Unions which now fill so large a part of the industrial scene. Liberalism has tended to oscillate between disapproval of bodies which seek to interfere in natural economic operations and concern for the condition of the labourers. The Conservative and Liberal parties tended as the century went on to bid against each other for the political support of the labourers, as we shall see. In the thirties and forties, while the Whig ministers were determined to keep the populace in reasonable order, the radical fringe was very much in schism on the Trade Union question. The stricter and purer theorists could see little hope in such kinds of social action. The more sentimental and crudely democratic saw the many and the poor defending themselves as best they could against the few and rich, be they landowners or employers.

We have mentioned the Poor Law as an administrative problem. It was also and more importantly a social and economic problem. The practice which had grown up in the Napoleonic wars of offering distressed labourers outside relief and even supplementation of wages was condemned later by all economists. It laid a heavy burden on the farmers, landowners and all ratepayers without giving the labourer the incentive to work as hard as he might. The new poor law, which soon became deeply unpopular, imposed on all able bodied labourers the test of choosing to receive relief and live in the workhouses, which were built by the new Poor Law Unions, or receiving nothing. The principle of this was the doctrine of self-help and the minimum of state interference. It was supervised by Edwin Chadwick but in fairness to him and those who worked on the famous Poor Law report it should be said that not all that they recommended was accepted and the "general mixed workhouse" which became the rule was a harsh and ill-devised expedient for so severe an operation in social surgery. Many were the satirists and critics of the harsh, skinflint, new poor law. Dickens satirised it in *Oliver Twist* and in *Coningsby* Disraeli has a good scene in which a benevolent old Whig Duke tries to make out a plea for outdoor relief in a hard case to his son, a young Liberal intellectual, and he describes the infuriated contempt of the young man for his father's sentimentality.

Historians have given very different verdicts on the new poor law. Broadly speaking those who wrote nearer the time regard it as a most useful and courageous operation. In this century the verdict has tended to become harder and harder. The best castigation of it is given in the opening chapters of the famous Minority Report of the Royal Commission on the Poor Law of 1909 which was the work of the socialists Sydney and Beatrice Webb. The practice of giving subsidies in aid of wages and for children, called the Speenhamland system, which the Poor Law Act ended was to the mid-Victorian the acme of economic folly. It is difficult now for a schoolboy who sees his mother draw her weekly family allowance for her younger children to see it in this light; she does not seem to have the air of an idle and feckless pauper. To those who live in the modern welfare state the nineteenth century poor law appears as an incredible nightmare. But that does not prove what it was right to do in 1834; there was a hard choice to be made between irregular and uneconomic profusion and the harsh and bitter remedy that was applied. The process of political struggle and social adjustment that has brought us to our present felicity is a long and fascinating story. And even now in cold academic cloisters voices are heard saying that the remuneration of labour in this country is dependent on forces which we cannot fully control, that however different trades and occupations may share in the product, the general rate of wages depends on the success with which the workers in the country and their executives can grow food, manufacture commodities and, by export, provide what is needed to maintain the standard to which we are now, perhaps too complacently, accustomed.

The move towards free trade was accomplished in several sudden moves. Only the third of these moves was carried out by an exclusively Liberal Government. Peel when he came to office in 1841 moved slowly by lowering duties on raw materials imported into the country but the greatest of all raw materials, corn, was excepted. In this respect the older Whig leaders like Melbourne were also agricultural protectionists. It took the sustained agitation of the Anti-Corn Law League to make further inroads into the surviving protectionism of the party. It took more than that, accidents of the weather. Gladstone was in his old age to remark to Morley that "politics are too much immersed in matter" and the corn law crisis is a good example of this. The terrible rains of 1845, "the rains that washed away the corn laws," brought distress to all western Europe, but to the westernmost and wettest island of Europe, to Ireland, it brought famine, because the population had become dependent on one food, the potato, and this suffered from a terrible blight. Peel felt that he could no longer resist: Lord John Russell declared his conversion and the way was open to passing the repeal by a good majority. This was the decisive battle but it was not until 1853 when Gladstone came to the Exchequer for the first time, a Peelite or Liberal-Conservative minister in a coalition of Whigs and Peelites, that a further leap was taken. In his famous budget of 1853 Gladstone removed most of the duties on partially manufactured goods and foodstuffs and halved nearly all the duties on manufactured goods. This is perhaps the best date for the beginning of a truly free trade economy.

In 1859 Gladstone returned to the Exchequer; he was still an enigmatic figure in politics but he was now serving in a purely Whig-Liberal Government in which Cobden had actually been offered but had refused the Presidency of the Board of Trade. And now, Cobden, instead of agitating from outside, had the ear of the Government. In 1860 Gladstone sent him to Paris to negotiate a treaty of commerce with the Emperor Louis Napoleon and the two budgets of 1860 and 1861 put the coping stone on the edifice of free trade. In 1860 Gladstone freed almost all articles from taxation as imports and only sixteen items of any significance remained. To promote trade with France he lowered the duties on French wines to the disadvantage of wines imported from the Cape or other British colonies. Here we see a problem which was to grow greater and which still perplexes British statesmen. Are we to favour products grown under our own flag, in the Crown colonies, the dominions, what was then called the Empire and now the Commonwealth? Liberal principles said no; the essence of the free trade idea is that flags and frontiers are dangerous and frustrating factors in the natural development of the world's economy. On the other hand the imperialist school ask what value there is in the vaunted British connection if it is never to bring material advantage? In 1903 Joseph Chamberlain made this question the prime issue of politics; he failed, but in 1932 his son Neville carried a full protectionist budget. A year later the Liberal members of that coalition cabinet resigned rather than accept an agreement negotiated at Ottawa to establish preferences for Empire products. Today the obligations which statesmen in Great Britain feel they have towards the Commonwealth has been an obstacle to entering the European Common Market, a giant free trade area in western Europe.

The Liberal free trade view in such matters, in its purest form, advocates the principle that political dominion is one thing and the organisation of trade and industry is another. In the complex government-inspired world of the twentieth century no one sees how this can be properly applied. But from 1860 to 1914 Great Britain did live up to free trade principles and held to them with remarkable constancy to the detriment no doubt of various industries, including agriculture, but with the firm belief that the total wealth of the community was the greater for free trade. Some forms of business, shipping above all, and banking and insurance, were especially free trade interests and many of the great Liberal families were to be engaged in shipping, Rathbones, Holts, Runcimans, Maclays and others. Those who sought to move goods over the face of the earth, to make contracts here there and everywhere, leaned to free trade. But those engaged in production of specific articles, manufacturers and producers, are more easily seduced by protectionist arguments; from their own point of view the case is often strong.

But this question is not entirely an economic question; the idea of trading under your own flag, of preferring your own commodities to others which may be better or cheaper, brings in the question of national pride. And so a moral or political element enters in. "Buy British" is a slogan that makes an easy appeal and there are many thousands who will instinctively buy New Zealand butter and reject Danish. The imprint, "Made in England," will tip the balance to many a hesitating purchaser. Liberal theory and sentiment is hostile to this.[1] It may seem harmless to prefer a home-made article to a foreign one but it may be only a step from rejecting the foreign product to fearing and hating the foreigner as such, in the end to thinking about war. The Liberal view was that protectionism contained a chauvinistic poison and was bad not only economically but morally. At the time that Cobden and Gladstone were negotiating their famous treaty Palmerston was arming against France, become more formidable by the opening of the new harbour of Cherbourg from which steam men-of-war, in any weather, would reach our coasts in six hours. This brings us to the interconnection between free trade and defence, a problem which we have known so well in this century. But in the age of Cobden and Gladstone Great Britain was so pre-eminent in trade and manufacture and so secure at sea that the issue of defence entered very little into the free-trade-protectionist argument. The needs of the armed services, the duty of statesmen to think in terms of defence as well as of national wealth, must however be discussed later when we come to deal with Liberal ideas on foreign policy and the development of the Empire.

[1] One of Asquith's last speeches in the House of Lords was delivered against a Bill to ensure the marking of goods as British or Foreign.

FOUR

GLADSTONIAN LIBERALISM

GLADSTONIAN LIBERALISM flourished most in the eighteen seventies and eighteen eighties. There was a precise date for what we may call its break through, the year 1868 when for the first time since 1832 one party had a majority of well over 100 in the House of Commons. The process of the formation of the new model Liberal party was slow and complicated and is very much a matter of the personal development of various political leaders of whom Gladstone was by far the most important. Of an entirely new Liberal Party we must not speak. We have contended in Chapter I that there was a continuous history of Whig-Liberalism from the year 1641. Certain families powerful in certain areas were impregnated with the Whig philosophy and continued to serve under the same standard. A Peer of very ancient lineage, Lord Saye and Sele, fought for the Parliament at Edgehill. In 1929 his descendant, Lord Saye and Sele was active as President of the Home Counties Liberal Federation. At this moment the present holder of the title takes the Liberal whip in the House of Lords. Other families, Greys, Russells, Dukes of Argyll, could show the same political history. But this element alone could not make a political party; it survived as an essential cadre to keep the party in being. Thanks to the split in the Tory party caused by Peel's apostasy on the Corn Laws the Whigs or Liberals were in a majority from 1847 to 1865 and the only Tory Governments that held office did so in a minority. The Peelites at times looked as though they might revert to their old allegiance but could never bring themselves to do so. What were the causes of variance?

To some extent it was personal: Peel's disciples and

friends, men like Sir James Graham, Gladstone, Cardwell and Lord Lincoln, afterwards Duke of Newcastle, would never forgive Disraeli and his henchmen who had put Peel out of office and pursued him with bitter satire. Partly it was a matter of policy: the Peelites became convinced free traders and it was not for a decade after the Repeal that the Tories effectively abandoned protection as a practical policy; many of them still hugged it in their hearts. On the other hand these men had been brought up as Tories and had a deep respect for the general conservative sentiments of the party. Above all they were good churchmen, some of them in sympathy with the High Church or Tractarian movement. They were repelled by the disdainful latitudinarianism of some of the Whig leaders, by Protestant bigotry as shewn in the Ecclesiastical Titles Act of 1850, and by the narrow evangelicalism of the dissenting Liberals. On other questions they were repelled by Lord Palmerston, whose forceful and boastful foreign policy seemed not only wrong in practice but wrong as ethics. On two famous occasions, the Don Pacifico debate of 1850 and the dispute over the bombardment of the Canton forts in 1857, they sided against Palmerston and Russell. Yet of the two evils, Disraeli or Palmerston, they came to consider that Palmerston was the lesser. And beyond Palmerston and the Whigs was another force, the radicals. These were now represented by Cobden and Bright. These were no natural friends of the zealous Oxford churchmen of the great vintage of 1830. But they had some merits and they were at least Christians; while amongst the radicals there were always anti-clericals and non-believers the staple radical tended to be evangelical and zealous for his own form of Christianity. The keen logic of Cobden and the noble eloquence of Bright attracted the Peelites and when Palmerston formed his last government in 1859 radicals, Peelites and Whigs joined together to support it. The two chief leaders remained outside the cabinet but were in habitual support of the Ministry and one of the leading Manchester radicals, Milner-Gibson, served as President of the Board of Trade. The combination had been formed; it only remained for Palmerston to pass away and for Gladstone to succeed. Thus the Peelites came to leaven the Liberal Party with a wider outlook on many matters and with their superb culture and intellectual proficiency. It took the Liberals some time to realise that in elevating Gladstone they had found a new master, a man who would delight, astound and frighten them by the intensity of his political faith, a St. Paul who, leaving the straitest sect of the Pharisees, would become the greatest expositor of the new faith, until the whole remainder of the colleagues who served with him weighed less in the balance of popular esteem than this one titanic figure, so remote, so virtuous, so austere, so far-reaching in his imagination, so moving in his eloquence.

If we pass from the high regions of Westminster and ask who formed the party amongst the electorate it is not easy to find an answer. As to the social composition of the party there is a generally agreed answer. Any schoolboy will tell you: it was the party of the middle class, and for once any schoolboy will be right. But, having accepted this most hackneyed of all political statements, it is necessary to refine upon it. It is difficult to say what constitutes the middle class. Some phrases which are little more than political short-hand are used. We talk of shopkeepers, but however numerous they cannot be a majority. Words like merchants and industrialists may also be used, but an industrialist may be a man of great wealth and influence or he may be a man who owns a small shed with a few rudimentary tools or machines. Merchant is equally misleading; it may denote a small wholesaler or some eminent man in the City, perhaps even a director of the Company of the Bank of England. If we go to Adam Smith, who like so many of the good writers of the eighteenth century was very free from canting expressions, we find the phrase, "the middling rank of society". The essence of the idea of a middle class is its medial position in a stratified society. Above it is the aristocracy, the quality, the holders of established and inherited wealth, and what is often more important, titles, power and influence. Below it is the class which we now call by the canting phrase "the workers", or sometimes "the people", often qualified by the term, little in use now, "the common people". The Victorians, who had their own fine sense of realism, often used the term "the labouring poor" and it seems as good as any. To be middle class one had to be below the aristocracy and above the labouring poor. The higher end of this scale is very difficult to define. Peel and Gladstone were sometimes called middle class, but their education was at Harrow and Eton, and Christ Church, Oxford, and their fathers were rich men who were made baronets. Later we have a Liberal Prime Minister, Sir Henry Campbell-Bannerman, who was also the son of a rich man who became a baronet but his earlier education at Glasgow High School and Glasgow University before going on to Cambridge, of which he thought little, gives him a more bourgeois flavour. Wherever the pure stream of "ancestry" and landed property was modified by some element of "trade" some trace of middle classness entered.

At the lower edge of the scale there is perhaps a simpler rule to guide us. We might say that a person was middle class if he was able to employ the labour of others. This might be domestic in his house or in his business, clerks, journeymen, apprentices. If he could command the labour of others he must have some additional wealth, what Marx would call some surplus value appropriated to him, as compared with the labourers who could only work for their wage and whose household must be run by their wives or daughters.

We say that the Reform Bill enfranchised the middle class. Leaving out some "ancient right voters", freemen, and others, this would mean men with a house rated at £10 in the boroughs of England and Wales or the holders of the nicely graded qualifications in the counties. Such persons probably did deserve the attribute given to them of being the "more responsible" element in the population. And especially if their employment of labour was in their business then it did make them responsible, in that they supervised the labour of others, they had dependents whom they taught and directed. If such direction was unsuccessful the economics of a free society would have their way and the employer would lose his business and status and sink to the level of the struggling poor. In History middle classes are always described as "rising"; that is what is observed and remembered. There is no chronicle of the unfortunate or incompetent, fallen from their high estate, but in Lancashire, where such matters are well understood, there is a grim proverb that there are only three generations from clogs to clogs.

We must not paint a picture of the electorate of the Reform Bill as a solid socially responsible and intelligent body of men casting their votes, openly, in public, with a solid sense of responsibility. The sad history of the long battle for electoral purity shows that for decades after the Reform Bill allegations of bribery of electors were often sustained by committees, and later by judges, as well proven. The battle for a closely fought seat often meant to the realistic eyes of the agent of the candidate some practices shady in ethics, contrary to law, which might come to light, often to the dismay of the more or less virtuous candidate. In many places, and especially in the older and smaller English boroughs, the old idea that an election should put something into the pockets of what Shaw was later to call "the underserving poor", died hard. In 1881 the ancient City of Oxford was disfranchised for a period while a royal commission disclosed the full extent of the bribery, while as late as 1906 the City of Worcester was, by a free, unwhipped vote of the House of Commons, refused a writ for a new election until 1908 when the House relented. Responsible politicians deplored this state of affairs and by various enactments and measures the trouble was at length stamped out. But this movement came from the top, from the House of Commons

3

itself, the electorate in general was strangely passive, only indignant when the other side won by unfair means.[1]

Included in the middle class there is usually what are called the professional classes. The professions are first of all the clergy, the ministers of the established church, the lawyers, divided into barristers and solicitors. There was also the medical profession and the teaching profession, at this time very much conducted by clergy. New professions were coming into being, Chartered accountants, architects, civil engineers and in increasing numbers civil servants, who now came to be thought of as more than mere "clerks". How far were these professional men likely to be Liberals? The clergy in England were predominantly conservative by their education and upbringing and also in reaction to the bitter attacks of the dissenters. In Scotland after the movement called the Disruption, which split the church in two, the established clergy became mainly Conservatives and the Free Church ministers Liberals. In Wales, where the Anglicans were a distinct minority, the clergy were on the whole Tory and the very numerous Dissenting Ministers radical. The lawyers it is harder to generalise about, but those who had the most established position and the greater income, especially those who were men of good family, tended to the Conservative side. The newer professions, accountants, architects and engineers, were probably more prone to be Liberal but there can be no rule here. And we must remember that class feeling is not merely a product of one's objective social and economic state; it is also a matter of imagination. English political life is full of examples of the aristocrat who chooses to be rather declassé and side with his inferiors; Villiers, the radical free trade member for Wolverhampton, would be a good example. Much more commonly we have a man of no family or position who chooses to be an aristocrat and if he tries hard enough succeeds. "After him

[1] *The Elimination of Corrupt Practices in British Elections*, 1868–1911, by Dr. Cornelius O'Leary, Oxford University Press.

Malmesbury," called Mr. Disraeli on the steps of a country house, when his Foreign Secretary had found that a messenger had gone off with the wrong despatch box. Young Benjamin D'Israeli had to write novels to keep himself alive when the rich young Gladstone was getting a solid education at Oxford; he had often to stay indoors in the daytime to avoid his creditors. But in the end he could fag an Earl. And for every one would-be aristocrat who by genius could make his dreams come true there were a thousand who could only dream, dream mostly but know the best people available and vote for the party of the best people.

The watershed in the history of Liberalism is the year 1865 when Lord Palmerston died and was replaced by Lord John Russell who had gone to the Lords as Earl Russell, leaving Gladstone as Chancellor of the Exchequer and leader in the House of Commons. It was apparent then to all discerning men that the effective leader would be Gladstone and his unusual character and mentality was watched with anxious speculation by the public. The Russell ministry was brief as was also the Derby-Disraeli ministry which followed it. Parliament was then absorbed by one question, the further extension of the franchise. These debates showed England trembling on the threshold of effective democracy. We need not here recite the tortuous history of the two reform Bills, the Liberal Bill of 1866 which failed and the Conservative Bill which Disraeli succeeded in passing with such radical amendment as to provide in the towns something like general household suffrage. The parties were both somewhat at sea on reform. The Liberals had to face critics in their own ranks led by Robert Lowe, an able Whig statesman who had lived in Australia and like many Englishmen abroad had disliked real democracy when he actually saw it. The Conservatives had no desire to open the door to a really popular franchise but were led by their leader to accept a measure which caused them some dismay. When the new law was passed and the new electoral lists drawn up Parliament was dissolved and the

result was to put Gladstone and the Liberals in power with a
majority of 120, the largest party majority since 1833. Now
it was possible to see what was the real nature and policy of
the new political amalgam which called itself the Liberal
Party.

A new slogan for the party had been coined, Peace,
Retrenchment and Reform. What did these words mean?
That peace came first was a sign of a real change. The Whig-
Liberal statesmen of the type of Lord Palmerston and
Russell were not pre-eminently men of peace. Certainly no
party in British politics at this period was anxious for war.
Britain was a satisfied power; to use a phrase of the American
naval historian Mahan, Britain was "gorged with territory".
She had no "national grievances", no terra irredenta to
reclaim. Her greatest interest, as Lord Salisbury was to say,
was peace. But this very security had its dangers from the
envy and rivalry of less fortunate nations. About 1860 France
had seemed to be dangerously militant; in the American
Civil War there were awkward moments when peace was in
the balance. And in smaller matters if the prestige of the flag
and the safety of British subjects was in peril anywhere from
the actions of smaller powers or less advanced races then the
mood of the people was to act with force. Palmerston was the
master of such policies. From the time of the Crimean war
onwards he was the statesman most prone to aggressive
action. To be a Liberal in those days was not to incur any
imputation of lack of patriotism. In a few short years this was
changed. While many Liberals inherited something of the
old Whig militant tradition, the party was irrevocably committed to the more pacific policy by the conjunction of
Gladstone and Bright. Those two great luminaries quite out-
shone the remainder of the party leaders. Bright was a
Quaker, a man to whose conscience any use of force was
wrong. Gladstone was not in this sense a pacifist; he had held
office during war and was as head of the Government to
authorise acts of war but the whole bent of his mind, the

force of his deeply Christian philosophy, made all such acts repugnant to him, acceptable only as dreadful necessities. Soon the phrase little-Englander was to be used as a means of insulting the Liberals. The critical, conscience-searching attitude to foreign and imperial affairs, the willingness to see the right triumph over national sentiment, bring out two elements in the thought of the party. The first was sheer idealism, the belief that war was wrong and that in the new world of great inventions and world-wide trade civilised nations should not require to settle differences by war. The second was the fact that Great Britain was a relatively civilian country with no large army; its great navy always remained somewhat insulated from political and social currents; and of the two parties the Liberals were the more civilian and of the classes the mercantile and professional middle class were least interested in military affairs. If fighting had to be done it was left to the aristocracy and its adherents who provided the officers and men of the poorer classes who from poverty or adventure took the Queen's shilling and enlisted. It was left to the twentieth century with its two terrible wars to sweep the whole manhood of the nation into the forces. At the present time most professional and business men over the age of sixty have been officers and can wear war-medals of 1914–1918, most professional and business men between forty and fifty-five have been officers and may sport the much more numerous medals of the last war. This would have been inconceivable to the Englishmen of Gladstone's day.

Retrenchment, the second word, meant the saving of the resources of the individual from the grasp of the state taxation system. It was held as a general truth that wealth left in the hands of private persons would be more fruitfully used than if used by the state. This assumption is questioned now when the activities of the state are so much wider but then neither party seriously disputed it. The Liberals however claimed to be the most capable of economy. It was they who from 1832 had most vigorously attacked sinecures and abuses; it was they who had established free trade which seemed the best guarantee of economic development and it was they who more than any others discouraged expense on armaments, the most wasteful and unproductive of all expenditure, on the assumption, a very big assumption and a dangerous one, that the armaments would not be needed to defend the vital interests of the state. And on the personal level they had the greatest economist of all, the zealous unresting opponent of all profusion, Gladstone, the greatest Chancellor of the Exchequer since Pitt, the acknowledged magician of finance.

Reform was the third word. This meant many things. It had a particular and narrower use as meaning reform of the franchise and the Liberals had still to establish household suffrage by their reform Bill of 1884. More broadly it meant improvement in the method and art of government and the removal of any restriction or disqualification that fell on any particular class or sect. And there was one part of the Kingdom where reform in many ways seemed clamant. This was Ireland. There there was a Church with about one eighth of the population established and three fourths of the population Roman Catholic; most of the land, the wealth and the professional direction of the country was in Protestant hands. This was a matter to which Gladstone was to dedicate himself. There was one kind of reform about which Liberals were in some doubt and confusion and that was what was called "social reform", their attitude to the "condition of the people" problem, poverty, unemployment, housing. Here they were restrained by their *laisser-faire* doctrines and by their deep aversion to public expenditure.

Gladstone's first ministry, from 1868 to 1874, revealed how the Liberals would interpret their mission of peace, retrenchment and reform. They kept the peace and avoided any part in the Franco-Prussian war of 1870. They showed their zeal for peaceful settlement of disputes by allowing the dispute with the United States over the British-built cruiser *Alabama*

of the Confederate Navy and the damages it had inflicted to
go to arbitration. This lost them much popularity, for public
opinion was offended by the terms of the settlement but a
desire to use arbitration whenever possible became a Liberal
principle and the *Alabama* settlement was regarded by them
as a singular triumph of international good sense.

The Irish question was tackled by a clear-cut act for the
disestablishment and partial disendowment of the Protestant-
Anglican Church and a beginning was made with the
improvement of the position of tenants of agricultural land,
the first step in a long series of measures to ameliorate the lot
of the Irish peasant, to which both parties were to contribute.

In the realm of governmental reform the work of the
Government was mainly to promote efficiency and reduce
privilege. Examination on a qualifying basis had been established for the civil service fifteen years before; now the award
of places was made dependent on open competition which
eliminated the element of favour and made entrance into the
higher grade a career for intellectually distinguished young
men. The principle has never since been questioned. One
branch of the public service was submitted to particular
scrutiny and amendment. This was the Army. How the
Liberals acted in this matter is particularly instructive of
their methods and principles and their limitations. Given
that the Liberals were the anti-military party, or at least the
less military party, there is something of a paradox that the
two great steps in Army reform have been taken by Liberal
War ministers, Cardwell in 1870 and Haldane in 1906.

It was however a natural consequence of political circumstances. The Liberals were indeed the pacific party but they
were not, except for a few individuals, like the Quaker,
Bright, pacifists, believers in non-resistance. They might
dislike the Army but they wanted it to be economically run
and they believed that it could be made more efficient at no
greater cost. But their lack of interest in military affairs
stopped them from making an effort to democratise the

Army. The professional middle classes who provided so much of the power of the party were determined to open up the civil service; they abolished the purchase of commissions but they did not encourage their own sons to a military career nor did they try to make such a career less expensive and exclusive. Competitive entry for the military colleges was established but the standard was not very high and the expense of an officer's life deterred many from that career. Professor Brogan has pointed out that the two great French and German Generals of the first world war, Foch and Ludendorff, were career soldiers of no means, a type less common in the British Army.[1] And lower in the social scale the supporters of Liberalism turned away from the Army. It is worth citing the opinion of an intelligent opponent of the party, Lord George Hamilton, for many years a Member of Parliament and later First Lord of the Admiralty. In his memoirs he writes: "Nonconformity had little, if any, touch with the Army. With the exception of the Wesleyans, the numbers from other branches of Nonconformity who enlist in the Army were almost infinitesimal. Socially and financially the great mass of Nonconformists are below the status of the officer and above that of the private. . . . Everything connected with our military establishments has for many years past been the butt and subject of ridicule of philosophic Radical writers and speakers."

If Liberals disliked the Army they also disliked the purposes for which it was used, never in those days to defend our shores but to fight in distant parts against inferior races. It was not so much an instrument of the nation as of the Empire. And as the white dominions of the Crown became independent self-governing nations the Empire came to mean more and more India and Africa.

[1] Lord Hankey in *The Supreme Command*, Vol. II, p. 820, observes of British and French staff officers, "There is much handshaking and outward civility but they do not really coalesce. The French are too *bourgeois* and the British 'trop gentleman'."

The problem was how much more of the face of the world should be taken under the protection of the British flag or left to its primitive ways, or, as was probable, occupied by some other European power. The Liberal view was that there was always a presumption against any further extension of our power. Yet these extensions went on, in Africa, in Egypt and on the Indian frontier. Some were made by Liberal Governments.

On some occasions action was necessary to protect British nationals and their property. On other occasions it was clear that if the British Government did not occupy some territory other colonial powers would do so. France, Portugal, Belgium, Italy and Germany all had ambitions in Africa. It was not a case of leaving the Africans to their own customs and ways; Europeans were on the move everywhere and it seemed reasonable that Britain should not always stand back. In the Liberal party there was always considerable tension between those who favoured an imperial policy and those who regarded extensions of the Empire as being at best a lesser evil than allowing others to have the land. And in many Liberal hearts there was a deep-seated conviction that the domination of one people by another on the ground of superior force and on the pretext of superior culture was at best hypocrisy and at worst sin. All through the population of Great Britain there was a division between those who gloried in Empire and found it natural and right and those who distrusted it and even reviled it. And this sentiment of hostility to Empire and to armed force was a subtle thing. On the face of it it was an ethical sentiment, for many, a religious belief, a part of their Christian doctrine. But as men are apt to deceive themselves and to be influenced by unconscious motives, the Liberal anti-imperialists were to some extent expressing less worthy motives in their sentiments. The armed forces were led and dominated by the upper classes; they had an aristocratic outlook and this was accepted by the lower ranks. The men who turned their back on such ideas were most likely to come from some section of the community which felt itself to have a grievance against the established classes; they were more likely to be dissenters than to be Anglicans, they were more likely to be members of the rising bourgeoisie who had not and would not accept the standards of the patricians. They were more likely to come from Wales or the industrial north than the metropolitan south except that in the great seaports imperial sentiment ran strong; seamen who followed the red ensign were apt to have strong views about the inferiority of dagoes, wops and niggers. They went abroad and actually saw these people; they did not only hear about them from returned missionaries and other philanthropists. The manner of a man's education was a factor also. And we must note that in the last few decades of the nineteenth century and up to 1914 there had grown up a remarkable institution, the English public school. Its political significance should never be underestimated. The word public may seem a strange term, for they were not state schools in any sense. But it is not meaningless, for it denoted a school under trustees and governors as opposed to a private school kept by a clergyman or scholar as a means of making his living. Some schools began in this way and were made "public" at a later stage. Some rested on the foundations of old town grammar schools and many were founded *de novo* often with a religious inspiration. It became customary for Englishmen who had prospered to educate their sons at these boarding schools. It was convenient, the education of its kind was good, and a bright boy could hope to prepare himself well for the University and a profession. But over and above its educational advantages the public school had a social merit, it was a cachet which would distinguish its product from others and open him to a freemasonry of public school men. The father, anxious to see his son advance beyond himself socially, would find that the public school was the best means. If his bent lay in that way it was the best avenue to the army; the navy, it should be noted, caught boys young at thirteen and let no other institution take any part in their training. And if not the army there was the University. We use the word in the singular; it should really be in the dual. For most Englishmen the University meant one of the two ancient universities of Oxford and Cambridge. And here we are in the presence of a strange phenomenon in English life. It is remarkable, although not inexplicable, that England, one of the broadest and fairest provinces of Europe, enjoying habitually more settled government and better internal peace than any other land in Europe, should have reached the year 1830 with only two universities, while Holland and Scotland had four each and larger countries like France, Germany and Italy, many more. In 1830 Durham and London were started and in the last two decades of the century the northern cities were developing civic universities. But in England there had grown up an institution called "the Varsity". From Tudor times onwards all "persons of condition", if their sons were not destined to a career of arms, expected them to enter one of the Colleges of Oxford or Cambridge. They would reside there, some would graduate, but the social atmosphere of the place was patrician and conservative. Poor men's sons were never entirely excluded, for there were scholarships and endowments for them. But in the period of which we are speaking the two universities, considerably reformed and revivified after their eighteenth century torpor, were an influence encouraging social, religious and political conformity. They always bred some radicals; after 1871 religious dissenters could become Masters of Arts. But in spite of this the whole bias and balance of the universities was Tory as was shown by the fact that between 1830 and 1914 neither university ever returned other than a Conservative to Parliament.

Now these developments in English education had a profound influence on English politics. They were on the face of it adverse to the survival of Liberalism. The period from the thirties to the fifties had seen the growth of a powerful self-conscious middle class, a real bourgeoisie with an ethos and spirit of its own. It was consciously different and in many ways hostile to the aristocracy. It had notable leaders, in politics Cobden and Bright, in letters Dickens and Thackeray. If this powerful class, growing in wealth and self-confidence, had remained a defined and self-conscious class it might have been an element which could have dominated the land. It might have created its own educational institutions and kept its sons and daughters separate from the patricians. It might even in certain circumstances have become republican under monarchs less ethical and less responsible and virtuous than Victoria and her husband. It was not to be. It was not in the nature of English society, not even of Scottish or Welsh society, to produce a third power in politics. The forces of tradition and of social emulation were too strong. Possibly also the middle classes were not wealthy enough, for while the wealth of the rising man is always noticeable it must be remembered that the aristocracy was very wealthy also. Their ownership of the land which grew in wealth, free from land value taxes and death duties, made them wealthier still. And if land was inadequate, by wise investment and prudent marriages they shared widely in the industrial and commercial prosperity. Disraeli writing to the Queen from the house of the Duke of Bedford was able to say that his Grace was "the wealthiest of your Majesty's subjects", his income being reckoned at over £300,000 a year. To this dominant class the middle classes naturally gravitated. The means by which this movement was carried out was the public school system and the Varsity. Minorities and individuals excepted, it was a system in which boys and men were taught to look beyond themselves and above themselves socially. Politically the effect was to make it natural for Conservative views to flourish and this became even more evident in the later part of the century when Gladstone had tarred his party with the little-Englander brush and to be a Liberal was to be credited with lack of patriotism. It is difficult to convey to the younger generation the crude chauvinism that the public schools inculcated. Some of the greater institutions like Eton or Balliol, might permit or encourage a certain disdainful tolerance, but in the smaller public schools and the smaller Colleges of the Varsity it was difficult, and it might be physically dangerous to appear as anything but a conformer. By 1900 the public school system was complete and perfect in respect both of its merits and defects. The intellectual tone also had altered. Dickens and Thackeray were replaced by Kipling and Conrad and a number of imitators by no means without talent. On the radical side the rising influences were beyond and outside the ranks of Liberalism, the socialists Wells and Shaw. The system of English secondary education was admirably devised to cut a line through the middle class. On the upper side were those who had acquired the public school rank, on the other were those, generally but not necessarily poorer, who went to grammar schools. There were also, for England never ceased to be an open society, men who by their own talents and efforts fought their way up with only a primary education. These under-privileged classes, to use an American term, dully resented the dominant power of the privileged. They resent it still, and recently a term has been invented for those who appear to have reached eminence by the fact of their parents' wealth or their privileged education. The word is "the Establishment". It is a vague term but not entirely unreal. And the Establishment was flexible enough to survive; the universities liberalised themselves well enough to permit and even foster Liberalism; they conserved their tradition well enough to ensure that the main body, the marching and voting troops, would remain or become Conservative.[1]

[1] The educational experience of those who have reached the very top of the ladder has in this century been varied. Of twelve statesmen who have kissed hands as Prime Minister in this century three, Balfour, Eden,

While a history of Liberalism must deal with contrasts that existed between the Liberal and Conservative-imperialist spirit, it is necessary to remember that sentiments and beliefs were common to both. One thing that is not so easy for young people of the present generation to understand is the confidence in the strength and security of Britain that was then assumed. It was assumed and with reason that British naval power would permit the force of the British state to be exercised in any corner of the world. It was assumed that the financial and economic strength of the state would make it possible to sustain a struggle if it were entered into. A strong combination of European powers might stay us in our course but no strong combination willing to resort to general war appeared during the nineteenth century. The deterrent to aggressive action lay first of all in the cost, cost in blood and wealth of any step which would involve serious military action. The cost in taxation was nicely measured and keenly felt, for the British tax-payer in Victorian times was sensitive to a degree that is now to us unimaginable to a few pence of income tax or the slightest increase of indirect taxation. (At the time when the Palmerston Government was hesitating whether to intervene in the dispute over Schleswig and Holstein, a German diplomat scornfully declared that Britain would not resort to war for fear of higher income tax. This was not the only reason; but it was one reason.) The British people in general and the leaders of all parties wanted peace and calm. But they could be moved to passion and resolute action by certain forces and events, by blood, the blood of British nationals killed in Egypt or China, the blood of Gordon slain in Khartoum, the blood spent apparently

and Macmillan, were at Eton; two, Baldwin and Churchill, were at Harrow. Two, Chamberlain from Rugby and Attlee from Haileybury, were from other public boarding schools, three were from city day schools, Asquith from City of London, Campbell-Bannerman and Bonar Law from Glasgow High School while two, Lloyd George and MacDonald, were from their local parish schools.

without effect on the hill of Majuba, and if not actual blood the threat of force or open insult would arouse public anger.

If life had to be protected, insults avenged, territory occupied and dominion extended here or there, the assumption was that it could be done. We were a great power, probably the greatest of all, although we never built up great land armies. And the problem so often presented was whether we should act or stay our hand. The answer was dictated by choice and not necessity. In Europe we had a general doctrine of non-intervention; in the American continent we upheld the Monroe doctrine which to some extent had been suggested by Canning and was a principle of our policy as it was also of the United States. But in the rest of the world there was freedom of action. What Britain willed to do was done. We did conquer Egypt and afterwards the Sudan. We did overcome the Zulus and in the end subdue the South African white republics. We extended the boundaries of the Indian Empire into Burma and up to the Khyber Pass. When the Chinese Boxer rebels had to be chastised we joined with the other powers in chastising them and added a naval base in Eastern China to our naval ports. If there was political dispute about these problems at home it was not about the possibility of the policy but about its rightness or its prudence. On the one side, in general on the Conservative side, it would be argued that we should be showing weakness, inviting contempt and losing golden opportunities if we were too mild. On the Liberal side, in Gladstonian times, it would be argued that right was by no means certainly on our side, that the hatred and envy which our action would promote would in the end redound to our loss. These arguments from ethics and from prudence could be subtly blended; both were necessary, the idealistic argument to satisfy the Liberal conscience, the argument from prudence to convince the less rarified spirits.

But in all this the notion of our power was never absent. In colonial and imperial questions at this period politics were the politics of patronage; we could suppress with a firm hand the hostile or dissident elements in India, Africa or elsewhere and patronise those who submitted and co-operated: they could serve in the lower ranks of our forces, they could hold clerkships in our government; where there were noble and royal chiefs they could be rewarded with honours and might even be permitted to stand before the majesty of the Queen. But the Liberal or anti-imperialist sentiment was also based on patronage. And what exasperated the imperialists, the jingoes, to fury was that these false Englishmen always wanted to patronise the wrong people, to make friends, heroes, martyrs of the enemies of Empire, to forgive and understand when they should have punished, to put the presumption in favour of the victims of imperial power. This is really a course which will appear patronising to those who receive this form of support and rarely will it go as far as they desire. The present age has seen the former subjects of the Empire receiving their freedom but accepting it in no way as of grace but as of right. These people are little inclined to distinguish between their former rulers and it has been disillusioning to many Liberals to find that, in the mind of the "oppressed", colonialism and imperialism, whether of the Liberal brand or any other, is like "the night in which all cows are black".

These reflections apply also to a country which continually raised the problem of the justification of dominion, Ireland. This was the one part of the Queen's dominions where there was a people, speaking our own language, living under our own laws, who felt themselves to be a separate nation and to be in all essential matters inimical to us. And Ireland was not formally at least an imperial problem; it was not part of the *Empire* but part of the *realm*. The union of the three kingdoms completed in 1801 seemed to most Englishmen, and not least to the more "progressive-minded" among them, to be a proper and healthy development. All the advantages that come from large units, from freedom of trade and ideas, from the opportunities of serving in the government of the great Empire and emigrating as free subjects to its varied dominions, all these were open to the Irish as to others. There were of course difficulties. Three fourths of the Irish people were Roman Catholic, the remainder fiercely Protestant. Those who were Catholic were with few exceptions the poorer people, the less educated and qualified, owning little land, eagerly seeking a tenancy in a land where there were more men than acres. To remedy these specific difficulties Gladstone set his hand. He called it his sacred task. At it he worked hard and well. He disestablished the Church; he reformed the land system in 1870 and much more radically and successfully in 1881. Then his opponents took over and the Unionists by various measures culminating in the Land Purchase Act of 1903, transferred the actual ownership of large parts of the land to the tenants. But there remained a purely political and national problem, a problem of the justice of dominion. Gladstone seized on this problem by his clumsily publicised conversion to Irish Home Rule in 1886. By doing so he shed a large part of his habitual supporters. These were of two kinds, the more traditional and conservative Liberals, often sub-titled Whigs, and some of the more radical and aggressive of his followers, notably Joseph Chamberlain.

But if the party which he led in his dedication to Irish causes was smaller, it was also purer. The pure Liberal doctrine of the right of people to self-government was admitted and applied to Ireland. But here again the element of patronage came in. The Liberals believed that it was right that the Irish should govern themselves. This right in a strictly limited form they prepared to "concede" to the Irish in the Bills of 1886, 1893 and the Act of 1914. But in their hearts the Irish did not want any concessions; they were asking for their rights and in politics there is nothing so difficult as to put any qualification on what men conceive to be their rights. The Liberals had to fight hard to get any form of Irish autonomy accepted by Parliament. Steeped more than any other in the peaceful parliamentary traditions of England, they could not conceive how a generous and considered settlement might not last. How Ireland would have fared under a Home Rule government in Dublin we shall never know, for it never came until 1921 when there was full dominion status, a thing previously not thought of. Liberals were prone to underestimate the violence and pugnacity of men. They were woefully taken by surprise by the threatened rebellion of Carson and the Ulster "loyalists". They did not seem to ask whether the Irish when they had freed their church and regained their land might not go on fighting for more. Did the Liberals ever seriously ask themselves how Parnell, or later Redmond, would have used the powers of the Home Rule Bills which might have put them in power in Dublin? Would they not have persistently striven for more power, might not even these two distinguished leaders be thrust aside by forces more extreme? At the back of the Liberal mind was the idea that the "concession" was theirs to give, Britain's to give or to refuse. And up to 1914 that assumption was probably true. In the stress and aftermath of war it was more difficult to maintain. It was not enough for the Liberals to give the Irish in reason what might satisfy them for the moment; it was not enough to show liberality to Ireland, to sympathise with the Irish cause. What they were unable to do, Gladstone and a few perhaps excepted, was to stand in awe of Ireland, to feel and understand the deep grained sense of secular wrongs, of religious and social subordination, of these intolerable "signs of undervalue" that make men fly in the face of reason, of material good and personal safety.

But if the Liberals were often viewed with indifference or contempt by their Irish political allies it must be remembered how much they sacrificed in offering even the half-loaf of Home Rule. Once again in Unionist eyes they appeared to be taking again the part of England's enemies, friend of our enemies, enemies of our friends, always with a blindness that was folly or an intent that could only be called treacherous, sapping and straining at the pillars of a great Empire, defended by armies which they had sought to starve and diminish, created and sustained by men whom they vilified or ignored.

FIVE

TENSIONS AND DIFFERENCES

IN THE last chapter we dealt very broadly with the general nature of Victorian Liberalism. Its greatest constructive work was accomplished when Gladstone ended his first ministry in 1874. There followed a period of defeat, a revival in 1880, in 1886 a disastrous split. Nor was the unity of the party really secure until just before the election of 1906. This was a period of much frustration to Liberals, and we must see on what matters they disagreed and what antagonism existed between leading personalities.

Many factors brought about Gladstone's defeat in 1874. The Liberals had accomplished much and like all reformers made enemies. Disraeli compared them to exhausted volcanoes. They had made new enemies in the liquor trade; they had offended old friends by their Education Act of 1870 which made a clumsy if necessary compromise between a secular school system and church schools. They had stumbled in their attempt to improve the lot of Trades Unions and left it to Disraeli to improve upon their efforts. Trade slackened and there were some bad harvests. Also they had failed to minister to national pride and the fact that this failure was deliberate, on principle, made the matter worse in the eyes of their enemy.

And in 1875 they lost the services of their great leader. Gladstone retired not from Parliament, but from the leadership of the party and in his place the party elected Lord Hartington, a Whig magnate, heir to the Dukedom of Devonshire, a man of strength and capacity but with little political zeal and no apostolic vision. Of the older figures, Bright remained, but by now his mission was more or less accomplished. Lowe and Cardwell retired into the peerage but Lord Granville who had been Gladstone's foreign minister from 1870 and was to hold the office again gave loyal and sensible support in the Lords. William Harcourt, a gifted patrician lawyer, was coming to the fore somewhat on the radical wing. But if there was something of a vacuum in personal leadership the party remained active and it was then, as in the Reform times, somewhat consciously the intellectual party, priding itself on its knowledge and thought and despising the less articulate and more intuitive judgments of the Tories. In the intellectual sphere John Stuart Mill, "the saint of rationalism", had died in 1873 but his writings of which the most widely read was his great *Essay on Liberty* formed a body of thought and doctrine which Liberals knew and admired. These writings survived as an active force. Dr. Gilbert Murray has related that he once asked Mr. Balfour why people always spoke of an "old-fashioned Liberal" and never of an old-fashioned Conservative. Balfour replied that the term was just; when he came up to Cambridge in 1866 he said he had found a complete intellectual orthodoxy reigning in political theory and philosophy and this was the Millite faith. Balfour reacted against it and resolved to combat it all his life but he had no doubt of its complete ascendancy at the time.

If there was an orthodoxy in Liberalism, an orthodoxy redolent of mid-Victorian ideas, was there any development or challenge? In the sense of an ordered system of thought the answer is no. But in practice new figures and new policies were emerging. Most notable of these was Joseph Chamberlain, the young Birmingham manufacturer, who from his entrance into office in 1880 to his defeat in 1906, had a decisive effect on British politics. He was then the hated radical who replaced Bright and Cobden, in the place to be occupied later by Lloyd George and more recently Aneurin Bevan. He was an activist, a man who demanded and secured action. It has been observed that he was a man best described in terms of the letter V, vivid, vital, vigorous, and his enemies would add vituperative and venomous. He had brought new life into local government by notable reforms in Birmingham and he brought new organisational strength into the Liberal party by a more effective organisation which he promoted with another Birmingham Liberal, Schnadhorst. This was at first the famous Birmingham "caucus" which spread itself into the National Liberal Federation. It worked out methods of canvassing and controlling the party vote in the much larger electorate and soon provoked the Conservatives to similar efforts of organisation. He was to have a strange destiny; at one time a likely Liberal Prime Minister, leading from the radical wing, he was to pass into alliance with the Conservatives to become their greatest personality and to fall just short of the highest office. With him in the radical period were John Morley, a Millite radical, a historian and writer of great talent, *laisser-faire* in economics, non-interventionist in foreign politics. He was to be Chief Secretary to Gladstone whose disciple and biographer he became, Secretary of State for India and later Lord President of the Council until 1914. The third member of this triumvirate was Sir Charles Dilke, a brilliant if somewhat heavy personality, strongly radical in some respects but with an interest and knowledge of problems of Empire, rare among Liberals, and much zeal for military affairs. His appearance in a very unusual divorce action removed him from the front rank of statesmen although he returned to Parliament and sat till his death in 1912.

While Gladstone sat in his famous octagon library at Hawarden, his country house, brooding on literature, philosophy and history, and above all on religious questions like the newly made claim of the Pope to be infallible in matters of faith, the Liberals observed with discontent the triumphs of Disraeli's great ministry. He made the Queen Empress of India; the Liberals said this was showy and shallow but the people liked it and the Indians did not seem to resent it. He purchased a large block of shares in the

Suez Canal; the Liberals said it was unconstitutional but the people admired a man who could see the greatness of imperial designs and act with firmness to strengthen them. Disraeli placated the Trades Unions and he made useful reforms in public health. The Liberals looked on sourly and some in moments of misjudgment sneered at "a policy of sewage". Their enemies seemed to have the wind in their sails. Then something happened. A revolt of Christian subjects of the Turkish Empire beginning in part of what is now Yugoslavia and extending rapidly into Bulgaria aroused public attention. This is not the place to recite the complicated events that made up the great Eastern Crisis of 1876 to 1878. These disturbances in an area of customary turmoil might have had little effect on British politics but for the fact that the two greatest men in politics were deeply concerned and totally different in their outlook. The Hartingtons and Harcourts and Dilkes might not have made it an issue and preferred a central line to promote national unity and, if they had only to deal with the Salisburys and Derbys on the other side, all might have remained calm.

But Disraeli not only had the traditional British view that the support of the Turkish Empire was necessary for our Mediterranean security but a feeling of sympathy with the Turks and a lack of interest or dislike of their Christian Levantine subjects and in these emotions he had much following in British Society. When the Bulgarian revolt provoked the Turkish soldiers and irregulars to terrible repression and massacre, Liberal opinion especially amongst nonconformists was aroused and in the quiet library of Hawarden Gladstone turned away reluctantly from his theology to issue a call for the defence of the subject peoples of the Balkans. His famous pamphlet on the Bulgarian Horrors and the Question of the East stirred the whole country for or against. By this course he aroused the ever dormant sentiments of Liberals for the oppressed and subject; he appealed to their humanity and their hatred of a tyrant.

He also, whether consciously or not, appealed to hatred of the barbaric and the foreign. In his most quoted sentence, with an almost perfect sense of rhetoric, he piled up the odious and outlandish names of Turkish officials in contrast to his solemn English. "Let the Turks now carry away their abuses in the only possible manner namely by carrying off themselves; their Zaptiehs and their Mudirs, their Bim Bashis and their Yuz-Bashis, their Kaimakams and their Pashas, one and all, bag and baggage will, I hope, clear out from the province they have desolated and profaned". But if there was some xenophobia in his appeal it turned against him when Russia declared war and the Turkish defence of Plevna won the admiration of British observers and when its fall led to the advance of the Russians to the Sea of Marmora. When in the end Disraeli was able to come home from Berlin with a settlement agreed upon by the powers of Europe his triumph seemed complete.

The controversy over the Balkans and Turkey is highly significant of the Liberal and Conservative points of view. The Liberals with Gladstone saw a question of right and wrong which they tended to over-simplify, they found one side which were martyrs and another tyrants. They had a simple principle, the right of peoples or nations, the two things are sometimes but not always the same, to govern themselves. They may claim that by 1912 it had all come to pass. Except for a circle round Constantinople the Turks had gone. The Tories looked not so much for right or wrong but interest and material security. They had some cynical doubts about the superior civilisation of the Christian Balkan peasants who were to be "liberated" and they had a genuine fear of Russian military power. The Turks are still in Constantinople and the Russians barred from the Straits. Turkey is now supported by western military strength. But the belief in the right to self-determination, as it came to be called, became more and more a Liberal doctrine and has never been accepted sincerely by the Conservatives. Woodrow

Wilson, the American President, who became in his time the great protagonist of self-determination, was detested by English Tories as Gladstone was.

Another principle was involved in the eastern dispute. Gladstone and most Liberals with him strongly denounced the failure of the British Government to work in agreement with the other great powers in bringing pressure on Turkey of which the rejection of a proposal called the Berlin memorandum was regarded as a test. Here we see the Liberals intent on something which was and still is one of their great desires, the desire to see a "concert of Europe" at work, the settlement of dangerous disputes by agreement between responsible statesmen; the same issue arose on a larger scale with the League of Nations and its successor the United Nations. Conservatives tend to doubt the ability and reality of such procedures and they forebode the loss of the right of Britain to determine its own course and follow its true interests in the shifting sands of international arguments.

If for the time being Disraeli seemed to have won over the Eastern question he was soon pursued by other difficulties. Both in India and in Africa a forward imperial policy ran into military disaster by defeats from the Zulus and the Afghans. Liberal anger mounted at the wrongness of the policies, at the bloodshed and the expense and the general public was embittered by the disgrace. It is the nemesis of a full-blooded imperial policy that it is always expected to succeed. Empires should always win, especially when they challenge barbarous or semi-barbarous nations. Harcourt in a clever phrase spoke of the chief agents of the government policy as "prancing pro-consuls" and this was hailed with delight. And now Gladstone returned to politics. He accepted an invitation to stand for the county of Midlothian, then, before its miners and labourers had been enfranchised, regarded as a safe Tory seat.

In November 1879 he set out for the north and his progress which was marked by episodes which we would now accept as normal; very frequent speeches, addresses at railway stations, great meetings in Glasgow and Edinburgh and later speeches in the small towns of the county, startled and offended his opponents. In March 1880 he returned for the actual election contest and in crowded halls, uncomfortable, dimly lighted, he held spell-bound the miners and workers who came to hear him with the loyalty of disciples. The image of Gladstone which was then established in the popular mind, as the old man eloquent, the righteous prophet, the friend of liberty and justice, lasted long after his death and was often more potent than the whole array of his gifted colleagues and all the party's nostrums and policies.[1] Gladstone triumphed in his county over Lord Dalkeith the son of the reigning magnate, the Duke of Buccleuch, and in the country as a whole he returned with a majority of 60; but reckoned with Irish support at over 100.

Now there is one thing which would strike a young person of the present day about this election and the issues which seemed to dominate it and that is the absence of material incentives. What of the great "condition of the people" question of which so much had been heard in the forties? What of the labouring poor, the slums, the prospect of unemployment and destitution? Liberals had apparently little to say and little to offer.

The fifties, sixties and seventies of the last century were times of remarkable quiescence. Free trade had triumphed and *laisser-faire*, never as complete as is sometimes thought, was at its peak. The way of political revolution by chartism had failed, the way of social change by trade union organisa-

[1] The present writer as a child in 1906 was taught to pray for the success of Liberal candidates (without the knowledge of his parents), by a nursemaid. She was the daughter of a Midlothian miner. It is related that in 1955 an old lady left her house in Shetland to vote Conservative but returning to her house for her purse saw her father's photograph of Mr. Gladstone and went to the poll to vote for Mr. Grimond.

tion was slow in coming to fruition. Compared with most other countries the people of England were well off in the perspective of the "short and simple annals of the poor" throughout recorded history. It seemed that there was no more to be done except to let the law of natural economic expansion work its slow, chequered, but ultimately beneficial way. This was the period in which the obscure German Jewish exile, Karl Marx, laboured in the British Museum and the first volume of his famous *Das Kapital* was published in 1867. It seemed to him that there was no way out except by total reconstruction of society; the temple of Dagon must fall. The rich were growing richer, the poor were given enough on which to subsist. It was not as simple as that. The concern of society for its poorer elements was never asleep. Much was hoped from the prime virtue of thrift. Gladstone, one of its greatest apostles, had in 1861 started the Post Office Savings Bank to add to the numerous savings institutions in the country especially strong in Scotland and the north. It has now 22,000,000, nearly one half of the population, on its books. In the same year, it was also the year after the Cobden Free Trade treaty with France, he had approved of the establishment of the Public Accounts Committee of the Commons, which still flourishes, to scrutinise the expense of the Government and to ensure against waste and profusion. By 1880 of the substantial Building Societies now existing 137 had been established, many dating from the forties. By them people could save and from them borrow to buy their own houses.

Much was hoped from temperance and Gladstone had, rashly perhaps but nobly, made enemies by his Licensing laws. About this time, especially during the decade of the eighties, there developed a movement which came to be known as "slumming".[1] Lord Shaftesbury and other

[1] The word "slum" as a verb first appears in the Oxford dictionary under the year 1860 where it means something discreditable: "to frequent slums for discreditable purposes, to keep to back streets to

philanthropists had for long been active but now it became
a much more general pursuit, almost a fashion. Young men
at the universities and public schools began to establish
settlements in London and large cities, some religious, some
secular. To some it might only be the payment of subscrip-
tions, little better than conscience money: to others it became
a dedication and was carried on through life. One young
Oxford man who went to the East End to learn and to help
remained to become Mayor of Stepney and to lead the
Labour Party to its first complete victory, Clement Attlee.
And while this movement did something to touch the great
problem of urban poverty it had also the effect of spreading
a keen and lively knowledge of the facts of poverty and the
possibilities of its alleviation. It should be remembered that
up to 1870 a great deal of the efforts of philanthropists
religious and secular had been devoted to education. Lord
Shaftesbury worked hard in "ragged schools", as they were
called and similar classes; so also did the young Joseph
Chamberlain. When the state at last took over the task of
national education people were freer to concentrate on other
forms of philanthropy. Sir Robert Ensor tells us in his Oxford
History that three successive Lord Chancellors taught
regularly in Sunday school most of their lives. In this grave
religious age Christian men and others laid burdens of
service on themselves. Was Gladstone an exception? By no
means. His most recent biographer, Sir Philip Magnus, has
disclosed how he and some friends formed a charitable group
in 1840 but Gladstone observed that it tended to come down
to signing cheques. They should rather devote themselves to
"humble and humbling tasks". He chose himself a task most
unusual and dangerous. He sought to help what in those days
were called "fallen women", the women by whom he might
be accosted as he went home by night. With a courage and
unworldliness that can only be called saintly he persevered,

avoid observation". But by 1884 it comes to mean "to visit slums for
charitable purposes".

to the dismay and terror of his colleagues who trembled lest the thing should end in scandal. They remonstrated, Granville and Rosebery tossing a coin as to who should actually approach the old man. Magnus tells us that in all Gladstone spent £83,000 of his income in supporting homes and individual cases. The sin and misery of this world was to him a personal challenge to be confronted privately yet not by stealth. He courageously brought to court a man who sought to blackmail him.

But in public measures there was little he could do by his lights except to make it easy to save, to learn, to work. If there was no great social conflagration at this time it may be because there was an outlet. Emigration was free to the United States and the British dominions just as it was free into Great Britain. Some of this emigration was directed and assisted by societies and the history of this is part of the story of the growth of the white Empire. New Zealand perhaps owes most to this. Still more of it was personal and unregulated; if you could save the fare or work your passage, lands of opportunity were open abroad just as chances of social advancement were before you in the free, perhaps too free, economy of the time.

After the victory of 1880 Mathew Arnold warned the Liberals that it would not avail them unless they tackled what Cobbett had called the "hell-holes of England". The younger men were uneasy but at a loss to see what could be done. During the decade there were stirrings in the world of social reform. In 1884 the Fabian Society was founded and those two remarkable persons Sydney and Beatrice Webb began their famous work for scientific socialism. In 1885 Henry Hyndman founded the Social Democratic Federation. The Trades Union Congress had first met in 1868 but the gathering force of Trades Unionism was not really felt by the public until the great dock strike of 1889 which was led by a future Liberal Minister, John Burns. But to the average party politician of the day these socialist groups were little more than coteries of gifted cranks and the Trades Union movement often seemed misguided if not actually sinister. Two trades union men with union support, Thomas Burt and Alexander Macdonald, were elected to Parliament in 1874 as Labour Radicals and an unusual Scottish radical laird, Cunningham Graham, entered Parliament in 1868 and expressed a sympathy with socialism of a romantic character. He was later to be the first President of the Scottish Nationalists and he exuded contempt for the middle class business men who were typical of Liberalism of that time.

Practical politicians, men who could hope to be elected and listened to, could suggest little in the way of government action. The idea, so strong in our own day, especially in the nineteen forties that there was something wrong with the "system", in leaving the work of production in the hands of capitalist *entre-preneurs* and the means of production in their ownership, seemed an idle dream. The Government was not considered efficient enough and perhaps not honest enough to undertake all these delicate tasks. Some nations like Prussia might have state railways, but that was an exception mainly for military reasons. All the great transport systems of the age, railways, steamships, canals, and even going further back turnpike roads, had arisen from the initiative of individuals and groups. So also had the factories, shipyards and mines. And it has been remarked that before the Government could undertake the heavy tasks which it now performs it had first of all to have the new skilled civil service open to severe competition which Gladstone had established in 1870. If it was assumed that the state could not successfully produce wealth it might have been urged that at least the state should remedy the inequalities of wealth and alleviate the lot of those who lived on the verge of destitution by doing universally and on a grand scale what men were doing by personal charity, provide services, amenities, housing, insurance against the troubles of life, by the hand of the exchequer. But this ran counter to the deep belief in the right of personal property that the men of that time held, a very different sentiment from the almost cringing submission of the rich today to the enormous levy made upon them. It was contrary for one thing to Adam Smith's First Canon of Taxation, that of equality, that tax-payers should pay equally in the same proportion. This was generally accepted but it is interesting that old Lord Clarendon, Gladstone's first Foreign Secretary told the diarist, Greville, before Gladstone took office, that he would not put it past him to start a differential rate of income tax. In the event this measure had to wait until Asquith was Chancellor in 1906–8. And if it affronted the idea of equity it could also be dismissed on the ground that if this country, in addition to supporting its great navy and smaller army, had to raise taxes for social benefit, the weight of this taxation would be a millstone to British industry and leave us helpless before our dangerous competitors.

It is easy with hindsight to daydream back into the past and think of what good things might have been done in the light of what we conceive to be our greater wisdom. The social structure of Britain and the system of economic production was a thing given and could not be questioned in any of its basic principles. Those who dreamed of a different social order, a new dispensation, had to construct their scale models outside reality and wait until the time was fulfilled for their revelation to become real. It dawned in 1945 and it seemed as though a clock had struck that would never be put back, although for many years afterwards it seemed as though some thick and palpable clouds are obscuring the radiance. From 1870 up to 1914, or at least up to 1909, politicians had to assume that capital would be saved, supplied and invested by individuals and corporations and that the Government would take in taxation only the minimum required for defence, administration, public order and health and something for education.

What then could Liberals do on the condition of the people

question? They could make useful reforms like Chamberlain's Merchant Shipping Act of 1882 which was a kind of factory act for seamen. They could establish and define the law of employer's liability, they could strengthen the system of local government as Chamberlain had done in his own city and as Harcourt did by improvements in the government and services of London as Home Secretary. But these were not matters of much party division. The Conservatives took the step of giving local self-government in the counties by the Act of 1888, while the Liberals in 1894 elaborated this by establishing parish and district councils. There was however one field in which the Liberals had radical ideas foreign to the Conservatives. They regarded land as a monopoly which had to be watched, a monopoly of wealth and power and esteem. The middle class still had its lively antipathies and the excessive power of landlords seemed a proper object of attack. Henry George had published his *Progress and Poverty* in 1879 and he visited England. This provided a new doctrine which seemed to give a simple scheme for social progress by attacking the land monopoly. His great remedy was a "single tax" on land to encourage thrift and labour. His work in part stimulated socialism, but for many Liberals it became a doctrine that could be combined with individual freedom, and single taxers became a sect within the party, a leaven which worked slowly but produced results in the famous budget of 1909.

Joseph Chamberlain threw himself not into the single tax agitation proper but in an attack on landlords. In the general election of 1885 he had his chance, for the last of the Reform Bills in the period, that of 1884, had conferred household franchise on the county voters and by a measure of redistribution gone a long way to establishing equal electoral districts. In his famous "unauthorised campaign" of 1885 he had wooed the agricultural voter with schemes for the development of small-holdings which were known by the cry, "three acres and a cow". He was successful in the election and many county divisions revolted from their habitual Tory allegiance. He went very far in speech against the landlord class; he denounced their rent and gains as "ransom" and pilloried them as drones in an industrious society, "they toil not neither do they spin". He attracted much hatred and the strain on party unity was very severe. Gladstone did not give him his countenance in full but neither did he excommunicate him. Chamberlain spoke in the strong general terms of radicalism, identifying the people with the nation as against the minority of the privileged classes. "I have always had a deep conviction that when the people came to govern themselves, and when the clamour of vested interests and class privileges was overborne by the powerful voice of the whole nation, that then the social evils which disgrace our civilisation, and the wrongs which have cried vainly for redress would at last find a hearing and a remedy. . . ." So far so good. But he goes on, "I do not want you to think that I suggest to you that legislation can accomplish all that we desire, and above all that I would lead you into wild and revolutionary projects. . . . But on the other hand I want you not to accept as final and perfect arrangements under which millions of your fellowcountrymen are subject to untold privations and misery, with evidence all around them of accumulated wealth and unbounded luxury. . . . It is not our duty, it is not our wish, to pull down and abase the rich, although I do not think that the excessive aggregation of wealth in a few hands is any advantage to anybody. But our object is to elevate the poor, to raise the general condition of the people."

This is the language not of an insensate demagogue but of a prudent statesman who is leaving the door well open behind him for escape if necessary. Indeed one almost feels that the orator is not so much trying to raise an army as to use a sounding board. In justice to Chamberlain it should be observed that he never had the chance in office to achieve any of the social reforms which he advocated then, unlike

4

Lloyd George who was able not only to lash the upper classes with the whips of his tongue but also with the scorpions of enacted measures. But clearly he is not speaking in the language of a Danton or a Marat, of a Lenin or a Keir Hardie, scarcely even of a Ramsay MacDonald.

Chamberlain, like Rupert, was victorious on his part of the field but on the other wing, in the towns, the Conservatives, stimulated by the audacious leadership of Randolph Churchill, almost redressed the balance and Gladstone in the new Parliament was dependent entirely on the votes of the Irish under Parnell. The story of his conversion to Home Rule is difficult and subtle and laid him open to charges of time-serving; certainly he was maladroit in his manœuvres. When he had lost Chamberlain's support and was defeated in Parliament he dissolved and asked the nation to vote on the Irish issue. Chamberlain's carefully garnered credit with the new voters was squandered away and he and other radicals never forgave Gladstone for this deflection of Liberalism from a rousing radical domestic policy. There had never been much sympathy between them. The Unitarian of Birmingham of materialistic mind was foreign to the High Churchman of Oxford, a merchant's son but a life-long rentier; barriers of class, of education, of faith and of age stood between them. It became, it still is, a general comment of some radicals and most socialists that Gladstone was "obsessed" with Ireland. The dictionary tells us that obsessed means haunted, harried, preoccupied. Any Prime Minister of Great Britain must have been haunted and harried in his mind by the Irish question. It is a hard fact of politics that where public order breaks down, when the personal safety of citizens is in doubt and when lives are taken, that will occupy the public mind to the exclusion of other matters greater in their material and economic significance. But Gladstone's concern over Ireland was peculiar in its intensity. Salisbury who had to rule Ireland for thirteen years said in his hard way that the problem was like the rule of Poland in Prussia, implying that the *status quo* must stay and that England would always be Prussia and Ireland always Poland. This was realism. To the Liberal mind a situation could never be defined in terms merely of power. They were often accused not without justice of lacking a sense of reality and their generous minds nourished illusions, one of which was that the Irish were more conciliable than in fact they were, that Church Reform or land reform would abate the nationalist frenzy, that a limited and measured autonomy such as was meted out in the three Home Rule Bills would be sure to satisfy the Irish and that under Parnell or Redmond they would quietly accept the boon conferred. Yet there was in Liberal thought a long term realism. Their political judgment told them that dominion by force was not permanent that to deny national right was to defy natural forces greater than any one nation or any one generation could recognise. While their detailed diagnosis may have often been wrong their general prognosis has been justified by events. The flag of the Irish Republic flies over Dublin (the post mark is Baile Atha Cliath), and Ireland is now styled Eire in the ancient tongue. Even Prussia, seemingly the most secure and immovable of powers, no longer exists even as a part of Germany and the Polish flag flies over the Silesian city of Breslau or Wroclaw as we must now call it.

Gladstone more than all Liberals felt the challenge of the Irish question. When first called to office by the Queen he pronounced that his mission was to pacify Ireland. And to the steadily growing doubt of the justice of British dominion there was added the very realistic reflection that without a settlement of the Irish question honourable to both sides the reputation and with it the power of Great Britain would suffer. In his famous speech before the second reading of the Home Rule Bill of 1886 he said: "Go into the length and breadth of the world, ransack the literature of all countries and find, if you can, a single voice, a single book, in which the conduct of England towards Ireland is anywhere treated except with profound and bitter condemnation. Are these the traditions by which we are exhorted to stand? No, they are a sad exception to the glory of our country. They are a broad and black blot upon the pages of its history." The odium against England, so general in American sentiment, was magnified and often organised by the hatred of the Irish. In the English-speaking dominions the Irish influence was a source of continual weakness to the bonds of Empire. And other nations, wincing under the moral lectures so frequently bestowed on them by Englishmen, found in the treatment of Ireland a perfect exemplar of our famous hypocrisy. In world politics the conciliation of Ireland was good business.

Gladstone's ministry of 1880 which opened so promisingly was to be bound in shallows and in miseries. These did not arise from social discontents at home but in untoward events in Ireland and abroad. In the House of Commons the Government had to face a new phenomenon, the Irish Nationalist Party under the leadership of Parnell. This daemonic character, one of the greatest natural leaders of men which the nineteenth century produced, decided to bring the wrongs of Ireland to the fore by making business in Parliament impossible. By skilful and persistent obstruction, ending in a record sitting of forty-one hours, he created a crisis. Gladstone, always a good House of Commons man, was reluctant to curtail the traditional rights of free and full debate but he was now forced to take measures to curtail it and with general assent he established the practice of the closure whereby the Speaker can accept a proposal to terminate the debate and put the motion for assent by the majority of the House. This proved effective and is practised still. There were limits to even Parnell's bullying of the House of Commons but he was effective in making Irish affairs the first matter of concern. Under Irish pressure Gladstone returned to the land question and in his great land Bill of 1881 he secured the Irish tenants' tenure more effectively than in his former act and, more remarkable, established rent courts to fix fair rents for holdings. It has been estimated that the average rents of Irish farms fell by nearly one third after this act. Here we see Liberals making an exception to the working of natural laws in economics. They could do this the more readily as the matter in question was land and the sufferers were landlords, always their habitual enemies. The immediate cause was agitation and political pressure, the justification was the lack of any equilibrium between the supply of land and the vast numbers of men seeking holdings. Land after all is in its nature a monopoly and that in the Liberal mind was suspect. The present generation which has seen for decades such interferences with property rights as our modern rent restriction acts which prevented increases in the rent of dwelling houses will see nothing very strange in limiting Irish farm rents. But at that time it was an alarming step. It is not surprising that the Liberals began to lose the support of some of their Whig members. Lord Lansdowne, a descendant of the famous Whig Prime Minister, Lord Shelburne, resigned from minor office and the Duke of Argyll, by his position the greatest of all Whigs, also parted company. While radicals and embryo socialists were complaining that Gladstone was too conservative in his respect for property, he was losing support hard among the landed rich and all who sympathised with them.

Throughout the ministry Ireland vexed the Government terribly and the Liberal response was characteristic, an affirmation of the need for conciliation, contradicted as it seemed by a coercion Bill and the imprisonment of Parnell. When Parnell was released after some obscure negotiation the opposition could set up the usual complaint of truckling to rebellion and disorder. Four men in succession held the office of Chief Secretary for Ireland and one of them, Lord Frederick Cavendish, was assassinated in Dublin which caused a sharp revulsion of feeling against any conciliation.

Ireland was trouble enough but the story of this ministry illustrates the remark that Gladstone made to Morley in extreme old age that "politics are too much immersed in matter". It is not enough to have the right philosophy, it is not enough to have a programme, reasoned and calculated objectives. Political leaders have to face the unexpected vicissitudes of life, to deal with the one-damned-thing-after-anotherness of human existence. And to a nation like Britain which has taken the whole world for its parish, troubles may arise at any moment in any part of the world. Disraeli had suffered from ineffective essays in aggressive imperialism. Gladstone suffered from the reverse. The Boer republic of the Transvaal was on Liberal principles to be given its independence. But, when a conflict took place between a small British force and the Boers at Majuba and resulted in a sharp defeat with casualties, the agonising question arose, should this event alter what was in essence true Liberal policy and, in the long run, true political wisdom. The Government took the course of living up to its anti-imperialistic principles and conceding after the battle what it had resolved to concede before without waiting to avenge a defeat and redeem its military honour. But from this time onwards the word "Majuba" was hurled at Liberals as being a symbol of their weakness, cowardice and lack of patriotism.

If South Africa and Ireland were not enough there arose unexpected problems in Egypt. What could be more utterly contrary to the spirit of Midlothian and 1880 than for a Gladstonian Government to lapse into the occupation of the land of the Pharaohs, the great valley of the Nile? But yet it happened. A nationalist rising in Egypt threatened British property and lives. It also offended Gladstone and strict financiers by its disregard of financial obligations freely contracted. France and Britain were the countries interested and with military power available. There was a bombardment of Alexandria and the rebellion was suppressed on land by a British force. So the men who had set out on a crusade against imperialism found themselves occupying Egypt and the Sudan.

For such a paradox there must be an explanation. We have already seen that British power made possible such intervention. If European lives and property were in danger then even Liberal anti-imperialists could hardly refuse to act when action was possible. British subjects had at least as much right to be protected from massacre by Moslems as Bulgarians. Liberal theory liked such action to be on more than a national basis. Gladstone above all welcomed any form of "concert". In the Egyptian affair the French did briefly join in, only to withdraw later leaving to the British all the credit, all the strategic and material benefits, and all the odium. But when Egypt, the lower Nile Valley, was secured, as it was thought for a temporary pacification and occupation, there arose another danger. A fervid dervish movement of Moslem fanaticism arose from the Sudan and threatened to sweep into Egypt proper. The British forces which had occupied Egypt and defeated and discredited the local Egyptian forces, could hardly fail to defend the country which they had occupied. There seemed no doubt that the Sudanese fanatics were dangerous "barbarians". Now the British and in general the white nations of the world had no doubt at that time of the superiority of their civilisation. What was at issue was whether its influence should extend by force or by peaceful persuasion and example. The non-white races were nicely graded according to the colour of their skins. Of the Indians and the Chinese, and of the Japanese just moving into the light of world politics, it was admitted that they had "very great civilisations" learned, artistic, elaborate, in their heathen way. Beyond them were the "natives" the pure barbarian races. One might leave them to wallow in their timeless turmoil. One might set out to civilise them by the Gospel, by a Livingstone. One might civilise them by force of arms. We had learned that we must not permit them to be kidnapped as slaves. By 1806 that was on the British Statute Book. By 1833 we had enacted that they should not be held in slavery anywhere in the King's dominions. We felt obliged to stop them enslaving each other by force where we found slave-trading in practice. Missionaries, administrators, soldiers, would all join in this good work and the distinction between these three categories were often blurred. This was a grave interference with the sovereign rights of the tribes and communities concerned. Influence was used to stop the slave trade in Zanzibar, but *Punch* published a cartoon of Disraeli expostulating to the Sultan who listened respectfully but added, "Remember, Conservative Party very strong in Zanzibar." Eventually the High Altar of the Anglican Cathedral of Zanzibar was erected and consecrated on the exact site of the old slave market. But still Anglicanism is not the religion of the people of Zanzibar.

Now the English Liberals were of all people the most averse to violence and force and cruelty. The militaristic and the imperialistic had fewer illusions about the possibility of the march of progress and civilisation. With what may have been callousness and cynicism, or possibly a more sensible perspective of the endless suffering that fills the continuum of human history, they were more inclined to accept as inevitable so many of the horrors that were to be found in the world. Where barbarism threatened within their own orbits they could and would deal with it, Pathans, Zulus, dervishes. They were also skilful in using the races of intermediate civilisation, as they were thought, warlike races capable of discipline, as their instruments. Above all they respected the Moslems, the peoples of the Koran, men of the Book, who for some generations served in India and elsewhere as the sergeant-majors of Empire. It is in our day that they have insisted on commissioned rank, as men and as nations. Home-keeping, home-loving English Liberals disliked this and did not sympathise with it much. And their fury against the Moslem Turks in the Eastern Crisis of 1876–78 was most embarrassing to the Government of India with its millions of Moslem subjects.

Liberals least of all men could tolerate barbarians and

barbarism; all their sentiments and principles were against this. Only an occasional eccentric, like Labouchère or Cunningham Graham, could say flatly that he did not consider less developed races less virtuous and less happy and that it was sheer impertinence to interfere with them. So it was hard not to assent to some action for the protection of a more civilised region such as Egypt against the Sudan. And when the test came and British lives had to be sacrificed they were unlikely to be Liberal lives. A specialised, self-chosen element of the population filled the armed forces and on them fell the burden of vindicating civilisation, of the defence against barbarism. Warfare, however just and noble its ends, implies a disrespect for life. The famous cry of Frederick the Great to his breaking troops, "Dogs, would you live for ever?" is not what one would call a Liberal sentiment but in a sense it is the spirit in which all battles are conducted. Once a Liberal Government had been projected on a military course, however reluctantly, they were bound to persevere, uneasily conscious that the forces they employed were in general hostile to them in opinion and distrustful of their leadership. Operations initiated by the Conservatives might be dismissed as the work of "prancing pro-consuls", but operations sanctioned by Gladstone could only arise from hard necessity and armies once committed must be sustained.

So much for the general paradox of Liberal intervention in Egypt. The actual events are an example of special and personal factors producing unexpected difficulty, of politics being "immersed in matter". Yielding to popular and journalist pressure the Government appointed General Gordon who had won a reputation for heroism and self-lessness in China and Africa, a resolute extirpator of slave trade and other evil practices. If war had to be waged for the defence of Egypt it seemed good to trust the command to one whom all recognised as a hero and some as a saint. It would probably have been better to have had in command a more orthodox soldier, less prone to use his own judgment and

4*

more apt to work within the limits of his instructions. The military appreciation of the situation was that the Sudan could not at that time be defended. But Gordon resolved to stay in Khartoum and defend it. He appealed for help from home but it came too late and Gordon was killed in Khartoum. This was a deep wound to the Liberals and in the years to follow they had to engage in tortured apologetics which cut but little ice. There was a case for Gladstone and a case against Gordon but Gladstone was alive and thriving, Gordon was heroically dead. There was general execration and in army messes and such places the letters G.O.M., Grand Old Man, by which Gladstone was often known, were transposed to M.O.G., murderer of Gordon. None but the most eccentric and defiant of anti-imperialists could do anything but deplore and apologise. Such a one was Wilfred Scawen Blunt, the diarist and writer, who protected by rank and wealth adhered to the most extreme anti-imperialistic opinions. Lord Hardinge, future Viceroy of India, then a young diplomatist, was staying with Blunt in his country house on the evening the news arrived. He was so shocked by Blunt's unconcealed pleasure at the news that he left next morning before breakfast.

With the Liberal move to Home Rule splitting the party and with Chamberlain's radical campaign abandoned and its leader lost, there followed a period during which the balance was tilted against Liberalism and the party was out of office except for the three precarious years from 1892 to 1895 when Gladstone again exhausted the energies of the Party in his second Home Rule Bill. This, as all expected, was thrown out by the Lords by a ten to one majority. During all this time the essential issues of British politics changed but little. The survival of Gladstone the Peelite, the man whose first budget had startled the country in 1853, the convinced apostle of *laisser-faire* and rigid economy, prevented a rapid move towards a radical social policy, even if, which was unlikely, a sufficient mass of middle class Liberals could have stomached it. The nonconformists were stopped short in what they hoped might be a move towards disestablishment and educational equality by this lofty High Churchman who, while minister in residence at Balmoral, had ordered a carriage to take him to Sunday service in a distant episcopalian church rather than worship by the Presbyterian rite in the house of his Sovereign. They admired him with generous enthusiasm; he learned to respect their Liberal and Christian convictions but allies in religious policy they could not be. He was the Captain and he set the course. It was still steady, justice for Ireland, come fair weather or come foul. And in this cause he was able to enlist and keep faithful the greater part of the most strictly Protestant sects. It would be pleasant to think that this was entirely an exercise in tolerance and the principle of self-government. It was both of these things quite genuinely but, since politics is also a matter of dislikes and resentments, the animus against the Establishment and the aristocracy, never more arrogantly displayed than by the Irish Ascendancy class, gave nonconformists a motive for venting their dislike of aristocracy. The Irish might be deluded papists, "wafer-worshippers", but they were poor, they were peasants, they were "the people". And also the Liberals under Gladstone came to recognise that Ireland was also quite recognisably a nation. The schism of 1886 produced strange fissures in radical nonconformity. In Birmingham and for a short distance around the power of the great Joe Chamberlain supported by the reputation of the aged Bright, produced a solid unionist block. In other places the Liberals in a great majority went with Gladstone, however reluctantly. In Scotland, where Gladstonian influence had been so strong, Liberal-Unionism became powerful. Possibly this may have been because in Scotland while there was an established Church with its enemies, it was not so magnificently endowed nor so aristocratic in its complexion. Also in Glasgow and the west there were large masses of real Irish papists, emigrants from

Ireland, deemed to have all the characteristics of their type, idle, thriftless, feckless, mendacious, superstitious, and, with their low material standards, dangerous rivals for cheap employment. The same was true of Liverpool and Lancashire and other northern cities. In these places too the Ulster influence was strong; the Orange Order was well organised, composed of solid and capable citizens. When they held their annual festival of the anniversary of the Battle of the Boyne on 12th July, marching in procession, their leader with an open Bible and a drawn sword, the band blaring out the famous marching song "Lillibulero" which at the time of the Glorious Revolution had driven King James II out of three kingdoms, covenanting and dissenting hearts could not but be stirred.

It was a wonderful achievement of Gladstone that he could swing over the rank and file of Liberals against so much natural emotional prejudice. But it must be reckoned also for virtue to Protestant Liberals that they could follow the logic of self-government and democracy so far and learn to grant to Ireland what they had claimed for distant Bulgaria. The famous Catholic historian, Hilaire Belloc, has generously recognised this fact. But what of the Ulster dilemma? What of the six counties of the north with their greater industry and better material success, the economic élite of the Irish people? What were their rights in this bitter question? In the brief flurry of the first Home Rule Bill agitation little attention was paid to this but there were some nasty riots in Belfast. Under Asquith's Government from 1912 to 1914 this problem will arise again until it became one of the gravest dangers that have beset our state since the Revolution. The slowness of Liberal minds to awake to it will be examined later.

The Liberal schism over Home Rule in 1886 is remarkable in that it took away supporters of two distinguishable types. It is natural to pay most attention to the defection of Chamberlain and his radical and nonconformist friends for this was the most unexpected and damaging blow to the solid front of bourgeois Liberalism. But attention must also be paid to the defection of the more conservative elements in the party generally described as the Whigs. This was a more natural event and many would no doubt have quietly gone over as the years passed on. If Chamberlain's secession was an explosion, the secession of the Whigs was a process of erosion. Some leading figures were lost. Lord Hartington, afterwards Duke of Devonshire and once titular leader of the party, was the leading figure. With him went Goschen, a wealthy man of finance who was later to serve Salisbury as Chancellor of the Exchequer. These were men who would probably have been pushed over by Chamberlain and the radicals, if these had remained in the party. As it was their secession was sudden and decisive; it was a damaging loss in the influence of great names, in wealth and to a lesser degree in talent. Hartington was a strong personality. He has been described as possessing a quality, which he shared with Parnell and Lord Randolph Churchill, referred to as "you-be-damnedness". He had endured much; he had been superseded by the ageing Gladstone in the leadership, he had to serve as Minister of War during the miseries of the Khartoum tragedy when it was judged that left to himself and free from the doubts and hesitations of the Cabinet he might have averted the disaster. He had been shocked by the unauthorised campaign of Chamberlain and the attack on landlords. The wonder is that he lasted so long.

But what drove Hartington to fury about the Irish issue was the apparent truckling of Gladstone and the orthodox Liberals to the bullying tactics of Parnell. He had seen him liberated from jail, restored to favour, courted by Gladstone only to cast the Irish vote for the Tories in the election of 1885. Whig gentlemen like Hartington were stiff-lipped people. Their Whig philosophy and traditions had trained them to live as a minority amongst the upper classes and they took some pride in their role as patrons of the disregarded

classes; they played the part of Tribunes of the People, but
they expected the tribunes to have the privileges of tribunes
and the people to have the subservience of the people.
G. K. Chesterton has remarked of one of the archetypal
Whigs, the Parliamentarian John Hampden, that "there
were no village Hampdens in Hampden's village".[1] But
there were limits to what such men would stand from social
inferiors who might be political allies, and Parnell's mixture
of bullying and, as it seemed to Liberals, treachery, exhausted their patience.

The Union was a tremendously serious issue. We have seen
that in many ways the Liberals with their Free Trade
philosophy and their belief in material progress were natural
prophets of expansion, of larger units. To go back on the
Union and to permit the rise of small inward-looking states
seemed a betrayal of general Liberal progressivism. Was the
development of the Empire and the civilised world not more
clearly the way of progress than the morcellement of political
authority to which the self-determination concept must lead?
Curiously enough both views were right. At the present time
we see the nations of Western Europe moving steadily
towards greater integration and those who talk of "national
sovereignty" being dismissed as reactionaries. We see the
two great land-mass nations, America and Russia dominating
the world as rival powers. Yet on the other hand there are
more independently constituted nations than ever before. In
1880 there were 15 independent states in Europe, in 1961
there are 21, excluding the various peoples' republics,
nominally distinct elements or allies of the Russian state.
There are more independent states in Latin America and the
Caribbean than there then were and in Africa new nations
are bounding into full-blown state authority. To the Conservatives and imperialists this presents no strain on their
philosophy. It is to be deplored no doubt in private, perhaps

[1] Probably the remark is quite untrue and Hampden may have been
vexed by insolent sectaries who refused him proper respect.

mildly regretted in public allusions, and Conservative Governments preside with marvellous civility over the almost unending secessions from the reality of the Empire contenting themselves with the diaphanous covering of "the Commonwealth" which, to parody Hobbes' famous words, is "as the ghost of the British Empire sitting crowned upon the grave thereof". But to the Liberals this choice between the rights of peoples to their national identity was a real political and spiritual choice. When they chose in the majority to stay with Gladstone they put themselves on the side of the small against the massive and the mighty. At the present time this can be illustrated by the fact that while Conservatives in Scotland and Wales cannot conceal their angry contempt for the nationalist parties in these two countries, the Liberals cannot fail to confess some strong fellow feeling. The choice for many was made in 1886; there are men now who may exchange hot words on some such issue but the decision may have been made when their fathers or grandfathers, close friends, near neighbours, working and worshipping together, parted political company in 1886 and walked their separate ways to the polling booth one to vote for Gladstone's man, the other to vote Liberal-Unionist.

And now from 1886 to 1900 we pass into a rather static period of politics. In domestic affairs there were no great issues on the surface. The Liberals, it is true, were slowly groping towards a radical policy which became evident after their victory of 1906. They had lost their greatest potential leader in Chamberlain. Their future leader in this field, David Lloyd George, did not enter Parliament till 1890, he did not really become well known till 1900, he did not reach office till 1906. And Chamberlain who took office under Salisbury in 1895 chose the Colonial Office where he was indeed energetic and creative, but this took him away from the work of social reform, stony as his path would have been working with his new associates. So far as controversial politics went there were two staple issues which aroused deep

passions and separated men from each other. These were
imperialism, which more and more centred in South African
questions, and Ireland, the urgent need for conciliation by
Home Rule or alternatively the urgent need for firm
government with material benefits within the Union. It is
in the nature of politics that there should be these static
periods when the average citizen becomes weary with the
continual iteration of the same cries and slogans, when the
reaction of the parties to any event could be easily predicted,
and all the time it was felt that there could be no fundamental
change in their strength. Those whose prime, active interest
was in party politics could follow the events and play their
allotted part with undiminished enthusiasm but a large part
of the public often feels weary and impatient with it all.
Such periods of political stagnation have occurred since. In
the period from 1919 to 1939 between the wars there was a
similar stand-still in ideas and issues. The great issue in
international affairs was that of how to preserve peace. The
two Left parties put their faith in the covenant of the League
of Nations, although their members put very different
interpretations on what action was needed by Britain to play
its part. The Conservatives in general despised the League
but had to accept it as a forum for international discussion
but put no faith in it. They looked to the strength of the
Empire in arms but were prevented by the need for economy
and the deep anti-militarism of the epoch in furnishing the
services with the arms which they demanded. In home
affairs the dominating problem was the unemployment
question, greater in its magnitude and more obstinate in its
endurance than any previous slump. The two parties of the
Left had different plans for attacking this grave ill. The
Liberals had a pragmatic approach within the capitalist
system. They proposed public works and deliberately
stimulated constructive schemes. The socialists, not averse to
such methods altogether, were bound to preach their long-
range cure for all social difficulties, the socialisation of the

means of production, distribution and exchange. The Conservatives pinned their faith in protection which they achieved in 1932 by their tariff policy of that year. How far the slow reduction of unemployment from that date was the result of protection or of rearmament imposed by the threats from Nazi Germany is a matter on which economic historians have yet to pronounce. And the basic electoral strength of government and opposition did not greatly vary. The two radical parties up till 1931 had a majority of the electors but as they could not combine the Conservatives were left in power for the period except for three years of Labour Government in 1924 and 1929–31. The electoral convulsion of 1931 was achieved by a coalition of Liberals and Conservatives with some Labour support. The basic strength of Labour remained fairly constant.

So in the period from 1886 to 1905 the balance was tilted in favour of the Conservative-Liberal-Unionist coalition. For one must remember that it was a coalition, and the Liberal-Unionists under Chamberlain and later under his son Austen had their own organisation and put up their own candidates, never however clashing with Conservatives. Deprived of Liberal-Unionist elements the Liberal Party had little chance of effective victory, for their Government of 1892–5 depended on the eighty Irish Nationalists and even with that had only a frail majority of forty in the House. Dramatic events there were in plenty. The Parnell Commission of 1890, a judicial enquiry into the connection between political agitation and crime, produced a vindication of Parnell from the charge of complicity in the murder of Lord Frederick Cavendish in Dublin, and this heartened the Liberals and made Parnell something of a hero. But the Commission also produced the most damaging evidence of Irish political terrorism, of whole areas held under threat, priests, peasants and all. It is doubtful if the enquiry deflected much voting strength from one side to another. Then there was the Jameson Raid of January 1st, 1896, a desperate, hare-brained plan to seize the Government of the Transvaal Republic from the hands of President Kruger and the Boers by a small invading force and an uprising in Johannesburg. Its failure and the capture of Jameson and his subsequent trial in London brought forth a storm of passion and conjecture. This has recently been brilliantly investigated by Lady Longford (*The Jameson Raid* by Elizabeth Pakenham) and there still remains much mystery about it. How far could Chamberlain, the Colonial Secretary of the time be completely absolved from complicity? What was the part of Cecil Rhodes? On the whole it damaged the Liberal Party, for the select committee which investigated the matter appeared to be something of a farce. Chamberlain was himself a member, judge and witness, the two Liberal leaders, Harcourt and Campbell-Bannerman, who sat on it appeared to have pulled back just when they might have secured the most damaging evidence. The rank and file who were hot for the chase felt that their leaders had let the fox escape. On the other hand the Conservatives and Imperialists were not seriously damaged within the country. Jameson was made a hero and fêted in society. He was indeed condemned on the charges which the British Government could legally bring against him but the trial suggested that if the Lord Chief Justice who presided had not been the strongest of men, and a Liberal and Irish Nationalist and a Catholic, no jury would have brought in a verdict of guilty. As it was Lord Russell of Killowen was severely condemned by many barristers for his improper charge to the jury.

Meanwhile, we were not wholly at peace. The reconquest of the Sudan from the Government of the Mahdi and his successor was in progress. An officer of the Royal Engineers, Herbert Kitchener, who had made a reputation by his determination and skill, was in command of the armies and persevering up the Nile he recaptured Khartoum and brought the dervish force to destruction at the Battle of Omdurman in 1898. This was something to think about and to stir men's minds. It was better reading than the interminable wrangles in the House of Commons. Reputations were begun in this campaign: the future Prime Minister, Winston Churchill, fought with the Hussars at Omdurman; the future Admiral Beatty was winning commendation for his daring handling of gunboats on the Nile; this was the man who on 31st May, 1916 when he had seen two of his finest ships blow up and disappear in a moment of time made the signal to steer closer to the enemy. And if these exploits warmed the hearts of the more elderly what was the effect on the young, the boys thirsting for adventure, devouring tales, true or fictional, in the *Captain*, the *Boys' Own Paper* and *Chums*? Were they likely to grow up into pacific men, doubting the wisdom of unadulterated patriotism, careful to think of the other side, of natives shot down, of great provinces brought under an alien dominion, of the nemesis that might attend on so much national pride, of the dangerous jealousy or disapproval of other great powers, despotic Russia, superbly organised military Germany and the ever suspicious citizens of the American Republic?

SIX

CONFUSION AND RECOVERY

WHILE THE STAPLE of politics remained the Union and Imperialism, Liberalism was not altogether static during the nineties. In 1891 at a famous meeting of the National Liberal Federation at Newcastle-upon-Tyne a programme was developed which showed the direction of Liberal policy. One feature of this was that certain concessions were made to Scotland and Wales. The principle of Disestablishment of the Churches in these two countries was accepted. For Wales a Bill for disestablishment was actually brought in but not carried by the Gladstone-Rosebery Government of 1892–5. In Wales the problem was fairly clear. The established Church of England was established also in Wales but the Evangelical movement of the late eighteenth and early nineteenth century had brought about a great revival of Protestant nonconformity, especially under the leadership of Wesley's colleague George Whitefield. It was estimated that by the end of the nineteenth century the Protestant nonconformists of many sects numbered about two thirds of the population. The established Anglican Church was believed to be supported by about one third of the inhabitants. These comprised most of the wealthy landowners and had an anglified aristocratic air uncongenial and even odious to the rising political forces of nonconformity. In the first part of the century Wales was politically quiescent and conservative but as the franchise was extended the natural democratic forces of Welsh nationalism asserted themselves more and more by returning Liberals to Parliament. By 1906 the Radicals were to carry every one of the thirty-two seats. This body, articulate, eloquent and politically conscious, was full of resentment against the hold of the Church, especially its control of education in the villages. In the education settlement of 1870 the Voluntary, that is to say Anglican schools, had been permitted to survive and in a district where there was only room for one school the Church school had a monopoly. Thus the young David Lloyd George had to go to Llanystwmdy Church school but remained none the less a hot apostle of disestablishment. This was characteristic of a number of grievances, religious, social and political, which pervaded Wales and made it a safe area in most places for the Liberals until the Labour Party first in the mining areas and then more generally acquired the ascendancy.

Scotland presented a different picture. Basically Scotland was Whig. This had been settled by the Revolution of 1688 which had re-established the Presbyterian Church and this was confirmed in the most solemn terms by the Treaty of Union which enacted that the Presbyterian faith and method of Church government must continue in Scotland "in all time coming". The Protestant and Whig character of Scotland must be firmly understood. Not all the endless romanticism about the Forty-Five and Bonnie Prince Charlie should obscure the fact that the people of the Lowlands, the most numerous, most effective, most intelligent and educated part of the nation, were determined to have no Papist King. Prince Charles, or to give him his legal designation, the Pretended Prince of Wales, found scarcely more to follow him from Edinburgh than from Manchester. In the covenanting west there was no response, Glasgow and Paisley were fined by the Pretender for their obduracy and the County of Ayr could boast that from that shire no one rose to join him. While in some parts the episcopalian party that had supported the two Charleses had some following, mostly amongst aristocratic families and their adherents, Scotland had achieved a general religious conformity to the Presbyterian Church.

The official established Church, like all establishments,

made some enemies and there were secessions at various times. A nation naturally so disputatious inevitably produced some fissures, but they were usually movements back to a purer and more perfect presbyterian faith and government. There was no "Oxford Movement" in Scotland, no harking back beyond the Reformation. Now all this meant that the basic political ideas of Scotsmen were un-Tory; they were Whig and so provided a seed bed for the later Liberal development.[1]

The Church of Scotland might then be expected to be a Liberal force. But it was not. In 1843 there took place a schism on a question which had been grumbling since the Union, the power of lay proprietors to nominate parish ministers subject only to the approval of the Presbytery in matters of morals and doctrine, the Presbytery being the collective body which wields many powers of a bishop. In 1843 the revolt against this usurpation of ecclesiastical powers by irresponsible laymen, as they often seemed, came to a head and when the Government of Sir Robert Peel refused to give legal satisfaction to the objectors rather less than one half of the clergy walked out of the General Assembly to form a new Church to be called the Free Church of Scotland. In a year or two they had raised one and a quarter million pounds sterling to build new churches and endow them, and from this time until the union of the Churches in 1929 there were two more or less co-equal bodies of Presbyterians in Scotland. Scotsmen generally take pride in this remarkable effort of independence and self-help in the name of a principle, but Lord Shaftesbury (Lord Ashley at that time) noted in his diary sourly that in this year

[1] In a famous passage in *Redgauntlet* by Sir Walter Scott, in "Weary Willie's Tale", the narrator in his vision of the damned in Hell pictures as one of the most deserving sufferers "the man who took Argyll", that is the man who arrested the Duke of Argyll in Renfrewshire on his effort to support the Monmouth Rebellion in England. This was basic folklore in Scotland.

1843 there had been a great movement in Scotland sup-
posedly in the name of religion but really for democracy. It
is not the whole truth but it contains much truth and the
Free Church with other bodies that had seceded formed an
opposition to the Established Church which had political
significance. This conflict does not compare with the deeper
animosities between the Welsh nonconformists and the
Anglicans, still less with the gulf between Irish Catholics and
Protestants, but it was there. Asquith in his first contest in
East Fife in 1886 noted of the Established Church with the
patronising amusement of a Balliol scholar, that "the old
lady had quite a lot of kick in her".

In placing these disestablishment items on the programme
to satisfy Welsh and Scottish Liberals we may observe a
somewhat ominous phenomenon. The Liberals were now
much concerned to look for support outside England. Later
the phrase, "the Celtic fringe" was used derisively of this
dependence on the extremities of the kingdom. It tended to
make Liberals seem just a little eccentric. For the South does
wield a kind of metropolitan influence and takes the variant
minorities less seriously. The English are wonderfully
tolerant of the other nationalities of the great English
speaking domain, at times indeed almost absurdly respectful
to Celtic fire and Scottish intellect, but at the same time they
cannot divest themselves of the feeling that these are, with
all their merits, comic variations from a perfect norm.

The Newcastle programme also dealt with proposals for
social betterment. Now when a body of mostly middle class
politicians reflected on what could be done "for the poor"
they thought of two different methods. The Poor could be
benefited by denying them things which were harmful or by
giving them things which they desired. One thing which you
could make it more difficult for them to get was alcoholic
drink. It was recognised that drink ate up the savings,
weakened application to skilled and regular work which
might deliver the working classes from many of their worst

disabilities. The diagnosis was generally agreed upon by social reformers. But the Liberals now prescribed a very drastic and unpopular remedy. They accepted the policy of "local option" which meant giving districts the chance to vote for the removal of public houses.

So in spite of the hard experience of 1874 the Liquor Trade was again offended and the great mass of ordinary philistine Englishmen alarmed and irritated by an attempt to interfere with their liberties in the way of drinking. Some of the defeats of eminent Liberals in the election of 1895 were specifically attributed to this issue. On the positive side a number of proposals were made such as protection of tenants against landlords, provision of allotments, and enforcement of workers' liability upon employers. This last proposal was given form later in a Bill by Asquith when he was Home Secretary in 1893 but abandoned owing to the wrecking amendments of the House of Lords. Gladstone gave his approval in general to this assorted programme of measures. It contained the seeds of much of the work to be done by the Liberal Ministry after 1906. It has since been thought that the Newcastle programme, for all its apparent inconsequence, marks the moment when the Liberal Party became not more but less of a *laisser-faire* party than the Conservatives. Disraeli's and Lord Randolph Churchill's efforts to provide a Tory Democracy, while still piously referred to, were to pale before an effort for something savouring of real social democracy at the hands of Lloyd George.

It was a matter of course that the Newcastle programme should also make proposals for more formal democracy. Plural voting, that is permitting electors to vote in more than one constituency, was denounced as undemocratic. And the creation of real democratic cells in the parishes of England was advocated. This was carried out by the Parish Councils Act of the Liberal Government in 1894. Parish Councils were to be elected in the larger parishes and parish meetings held in the smaller, and both on a simple ratepaying suffrage. At the same time old urban and sanitary areas were reconstituted as urban and rural district councils. These are still with us but it took more than a generation before all this produced any real democratisation of local government.

The short ministry of 1892, in spite of the time devoted to the hopeless task of passing a Home Rule Bill for slaughter in the Lords, was by no means without legislative fruit. But its prime importance is that it brought Liberals into power once more; it gave more experience to the senior and their first experience of office to the younger men. Without this experience of office the Party would have been in a much weaker position in 1906. Amongst the younger men who came into office then were Herbert Henry Asquith, a brilliant barrister who was given the Home Office. A young Northumberland Baronet, Sir Edward Grey, as Under-Secretary for the Foreign Office had his first training in diplomacy which qualified him for his fateful foreign secretaryship from 1905 to 1916. James Bryce, already a celebrated jurist and historian, also had office; he was to be a Minister in 1905 and afterwards Ambassador in Washington. Another younger man who did not actually receive office was Richard Burdon Haldane, future War Minister and later Lord Chancellor.

While there was no lack of talent coming on in the party it was much vexed by friction at the top. This friction was both political and personal. In varying degrees the Ministry was divided into those who were more and those who were less imperialist. And it was divided at times on Defence. The Chancellor of the Exchequer, Sir William Harcourt, fought for economy in true Gladstonian style. His fiery temper and blistering speech made him formidable to his colleagues. "And now I must face the blizzard", said the First Lord of the Admiralty as he left for the Treasury to put the Navy estimates before the Chancellor. It was not known at the time but Gladstone's resignation in 1894 which the public took as an honoured retirement was accelerated by his bitter opposition to the figure of the Navy estimates which he opposed to an extent that none even of the economisers in the Cabinet could follow him.

His retirement was indeed inevitable. He was now eighty-five years of age. His sight and hearing were becoming defective. As he put it, "the senses are closing in on me". But his last speech in the Commons before he resigned looked firmly to the future. He spoke of the inveterate interference of the Tory majority in the Lords to measures passed with the utmost deliberation by the Commons, and he declared that this was a matter "which must go forward to its issue". And now the great problem which confronted the Party was who could bend the bow of Ulysses? No one could compare with Gladstone in his moral and personal ascendancy, no one in experience, and probably no one even in sheer natural ability. There was one obvious man and that was the Chancellor of the Exchequer, Sir William Harcourt. He would best satisfy the more radical element, his experience was great, his talents remarkable. But there was that in his personality, his propensity to anger and sarcasm which made even his closest political allies shrink from having him as leader. Gladstone was well aware of this and favoured a peer, Lord Spencer, who had been Viceroy of Ireland and was one of the few high Whigs who had stuck to him in 1886.

However it was not for the Party to decide. Queen Victoria had her own views. With what seems studied discourtesy she did not even ask Gladstone for his advice but sent for Lord Rosebery. This prerogative of sending for the man of her choice is still a prerogative of the Sovereign but it is understood that now careful consultation with leaders will take place.

Lord Rosebery held the Foreign Office and was by general consent a most distinguished man. Still young, he was then forty-eight, he had shown his excellent talents at Eton and at Oxford. He had taken part in public life in Scotland where he was a Scottish peer of ancient creation and had shown his

zeal by becoming chairman of the London County Council.
He was rich, talented, handsome, famous, but there was
something wayward in his character; the burden of politics
was heavy on him who had so many other interests and he
could irritate his colleagues by an air of aloofness. After
hesitating to accept Gladstone's brilliant offer of the Foreign
Office he acceded in a laconic telegram which enraged the
fiery Harcourt, who on meeting him at his first Cabinet
remarked: "Without you, Rosebery, this Ministry would be
ridiculous. With you it will be merely impossible".

His brief tenure of office was not by any means ineffective,
but when the Government fell over an amendment to the
War Office Estimates, Rosebery with the support of most of
his colleagues took the course of resigning and not dissolving.
Probably it made little difference, for the party seemed weak
and its measures were mostly unpopular. The Conservatives
with their new Unionist allies had a majority of 150 in the
new Parliament. Chamberlain was brought in to strengthen
the ministry and the Liberals were out apparently for a long
time. As often happens with defeated parties there was much
discontent and criticism of the leadership and the leaders
were discontented with the party and the party platform.
Rosebery did not stand it for long. In 1896 he resigned. His
main discontent, apart from weariness with the dust of
politics, was with the continued adherence of the Party to
the principle of Home Rule for Ireland. He disliked having
to embark with this Jonah aboard. Now at last Harcourt
stepped into what seemed to be his destined position as
leader but he too became discontented and asked to be
relieved. Personal considerations apart he was too deter-
minedly anti-imperialist to suit the mood of the country at
the time. The Party had to choose again and in their embar-
rassment made a choice which seemed at the time a rather
weak compromise but which proved in the end a happy
appointment. Sir Henry Campbell-Bannerman, Member for
Stirling Burghs since 1868, was elected. He was the younger

son of a rich Glasgow merchant, oddly enough a Conservative. In his youth he had taken to the radical side and entered the House by displacing a too Whiggish holder of the seat. He was now a man of much wealth, for he had inherited a fortune from an uncle and had added the name of Bannerman to his original surname of Campbell. He was a big, genial, rather easy-going man, by no means brilliant, a very moderate speaker, but shrewd and acute and a keen observer of the foibles and weaknesses of other men. Sir Edward Grey, to whom he was no friend, observed later, that he had not the countervailing gift of appreciating the merits of men. He had held minor office in the service ministries but had become Chief Secretary for Ireland towards the end of Gladstone's ministry of 1880 and had held that perilous office with remarkable calm and skill. In the last ministry he had the War Office and had shown much address in his handling of military men. He had the one great merit that if any one could calm the party and hold it together he could. For this purpose he had two qualifications; one was personal; he was a good humoured man of the world who could handle men and the fact that his experience had mainly been in the service ministries was some comfort to the more military and imperial members. But underneath, it was obscurely recognised, he had a firm base of radicalism, of a somewhat Victorian and Gladstonian type. Other more gifted leaders like Harcourt and Rosebery would have been in their different ways an antithesis to Gladstone. But what the faithful of the Party wanted was a successor, a continuator of Gladstonian ideas, and slowly they began to look with benevolence on the mild Elisha who had dutifully accepted the mantle of the inspired prophet while making no claim to fill out its voluminous folds.

As the century drew to its close, public attention became more and more directed to South Africa. There the problem of the co-existence of the more ancient Dutch and more recent British settlers had become acute. There were two colonies, the Cape of Good Hope and Natal. The Cape which had originally passed into British hands in the Napoleonic war, had a mixed population with a strong Dutch element. Natal was more British. Inland, beyond the Colonies, were the two Republics, the Transvaal and the Orange Free State. They were basically agricultural and almost wholly Dutch or Boer. (The word Boer means farmer.) But in 1885 gold in large quantities was discovered in the Transvaal and the city of Johannesburg arose. Into it poured men of many nations but predominantly British subjects. This alien element was odious to the Boers but the gold they mined was profitable. The ruler of the Transvaal, President Kruger, was determined to keep the alien element in check, for otherwise they might outnumber the native Boers. The emigrants, known as the Uitlanders, felt themselves persecuted and unjustly treated. They were denied full political rights and made a good case for themselves on this account. But the Boers were well aware that the British imperialists, who were led by the great pioneer, Cecil Rhodes, in the Cape, and had the force of active British opinion behind them, were thinking of more than mere votes in the Transvaal. They were looking to a vast extension of British imperial power over Africa. To the north of the Transvaal and its fellow Republic, the Orange Free State, were the territories called Rhodesia. It was planned to join up these territories with British East Africa, now called Kenya, with Uganda which the anti-imperialists in the Rosebery Administration had been unable to stop our Government from acquiring as a protectorate. Beyond that was the Sudan where the victorious Kitchener was moving southward to link up eventually with the British advancing from the south and east.

Now all this presented Liberals with a sharp dilemma. Was it not "manifest destiny" that this great extension of our power should take place? Could we hold back the blessings of civilisation from tribes sunk in hopeless barbarism? Must we leave it to the French, the Germans and the Belgians to

acquire? And what stood in our way? Only the two little
Dutch Republics, with a Dutch, Afrikaner, population less
than the two counties of Denbigh and Flint. What right had
a number so small to hold up this splendid and beneficent
development? Could they claim more civilisation than the
British? By no means; it was felt that they were narrow,
hidebound, unprogressive. Their religion, a form of Dutch
Calvinism, appeared narrow and unenlightened to most
Englishmen, although it made them members of that broad
communion, the Reformed Church, and similar to the
Presbyterians. Were they better friends and guardians of the
black natives? Not at all. It was notorious that in their theory
and their practice they were repressive and even cruel. The
way of enlightenment did not seem to be to encourage them
and to enthrone them in perpetual authority on the grounds
of their "national" rights.

To many Liberals and ex-Liberals these arguments seemed
good. If one believed in progress, in the spread of science and
knowledge and a firm but merciful authority, was there not
an interest and indeed a duty for Britain to become the great
colonising, developing, protecting power, and bring to this
vast area the blessings, material and moral, of civilisation?
Britain, supreme upon the sea, had the military power, she
could bring the capital, much of the élite of her educated
population were striving outwards; men with not only
careers to make but a mission to fulfil were thirsting to take
their place in this great endeavour. It is true that there
were strong material interests concerned. But there were
moral interests also. If Trade followed or very often pre-
ceded the flag, so did the Bible and the Altar. The humane
work of the missionaries and doctors towards the natives
would thrive best under a great imperial dominion. And it
must not be forgotten that the famous Trek of the Boers
northwards from the Cape which had formed the Transvaal
and Orange Free State had been provoked by the Boers'
hostility to the methods of the English missionaries to the

natives. The Liberal and Radical elements in the country were inevitably torn one way or the other by these considerations. In the rising movement of the Fabian Socialists also the strain was felt. The Memoirs of Beatrice Webb reveal how much she and her husband were perplexed by this and how like other "scientific socialists" they could hardly give their blessing to the "reactionary Kruger". Bernard Shaw also had the same view. Amongst Liberals it is worth observing that Haldane who could claim to be a scientific politician was the least hostile to the imperialist designs; Rosebery a man widely travelled in the Empire was also on the imperialist side and with him, more moderately, Asquith and Grey. And these were the younger elements in the Party. On the other side Harcourt was old, Campbell-Bannerman elderly, Bryce also senior. Might not the call of the future be towards a balanced and constructive view of Empire unimpeded by the brooding doubts of Gladstone, the uncompromising isolationism of Cobden and the quakerish intransigence of Bright? But in addition to these very rational and proper arguments one must consider what one can only call the set or mood of English society, those assumptions, beliefs, ideas and enthusiasms which were general and natural amongst the dominating and directing elements of the nation. As far back as the reign of Queen Anne the Tory thinker and statesman, Bolingbroke, had stigmatised the political ideas of the Whigs as "unnatural". "Observe" he writes to his colleague, Harley, "the difference between the true strength of this *nation* and the fictitious one of the whigs". (Feiling, *History of the Tory Party*, p. 388.) The idea that Liberal policy ran counter to the natural sentiments of the nation was still strong, perhaps as strong as ever. The imperial and "patriotic" ideas were the more normal. The great mass of fiction with which all reading people amused themselves illustrate this abundantly. It is true that with the end of the century the greatest figures in literature were not Conservative, Kipling and Conrad excepted. Wells' brilliant scientific and social novels were a continuous critique of society and education as it stood. Shaw with his plays and prefaces was a profound influence on the socialist side. Chesterton and Belloc, coming into prominence, were Catholic-Liberal romantics. Arnold Bennett was the epitome of middle class Liberal conceptions however cleverly he satirised his Methodist upbringing. But it is often more important to study not the great figures whose books are a very slow-working leaven, but to consider the average novelist, and there were many good ones of the second rank, whose books were in all the circulating libraries and which reveal so clearly what the average, usually middle class reader was expected to like and sympathise with.

A good example of these is the work of John Buchan, a very capable and gifted writer, afterwards Lord Tweedsmuir and Governor-General of Canada. He was the son of a Presbyterian minister in Glasgow, actually a Free Church minister. From there he went to Oxford and became a most prolific writer not only in fiction. He served on Lord Milner's staff on his mission to South Africa. His novels of adventure which are admirable of their kind, show his heroes and leading characters as broad-minded men of the world, liberal with a small l, familiar with the lands of the Empire but returning to London to talk over in their clubs their hazardous and eventually successful exploits. They are generally persons of condition, moderately affluent, some military, all of them virile and brave, tolerant of different classes and races but made of steel when an enemy of Britain is to be overcome. In one particularly brilliant story, *Prester John*, he tells of the rise and fall of a gifted black man who has learned much of the wisdom of the west and who hopes himself to revive a great black Empire over Africa. Now the tone of these novels of which John Buchan's are distinguished examples was general, indeed almost universal. The favoured figures are in a broad way Tory, imperialistic, not narrow-minded bullying squires or didactic parsons but men whom one can admire and whose conduct and views conform to a norm that readers were expected to like and to model themselves on. It is not very different now. Take up any average detective novel designed for wide if not mass circulation and the characteristics of a John Buchan hero are usually apparent. In the last decade no doubt a change has come but these stereotypes of fiction are of great political significance. Their reign was long and indeed it was glorious. While the terrible death roll of the two wars cut through all classes, many of the most distinguished figures whose exploits were most celebrated and brilliant come from such a class.

We must never therefore forget how hard it was for the ordinary Liberal to remain immune from the prevailing imperialistic frame of mind. As Liberals are apt to be consciously superior ethically and intellectually they would be restrained by their political beliefs from falling into the worst excesses of jingoism. They tried hard, they tried genuinely, to see both sides. But it was natural to settle for a modified and critical version of the gospel of Empire which came to be known as Liberal Imperialism. To go the whole hog on the anti-imperialist line was difficult, it led to trouble in social life, it might be disadvantageous to your career, it required much fortitude or else a very thick skin; or it might be harboured in a close environment of a small set or small religious group. Of these perhaps the Quakers were the most secure.

And yet the Liberals retained in their heart a strong element of deep anti-imperial sentiment and doctrine. One factor in this was the Jameson Raid of 1896. This wicked and ridiculous attempt on a state recognised by our Government as independent in all save foreign policy was a stumbling block to all the arguments that the imperialists could put up to justify a forward policy in South Africa. It gave, or ought to have given, the imperialists a bad conscience. But what gives the imperialists and jingoes a bad conscience gives the Liberals a good conscience. When you came to regret,

5

deplore, abhor, the South African war of 1899 to 1902 you could always say that the Jameson Raid had put us in the wrong. Jameson was at last a counter cry to the jeering Conservative cry of "Majuba". That such an act could provoke so much sympathy, so much admiration, so much delight in the attempt, so much regret at the failure, seemed to cover the imperial designs in South Africa with disgrace, with infamy, there were those who would say quite boldly with sin. The Raid over, Jameson surrendered, arrested, tried, condemned, imprisoned, released and glorified, attention turned to the South African problem as it then stood. Two of the very ablest men in the political service of Britain directed affairs. The Colonial Secretary was Joseph Chamberlain and from 1897 the High Commissioner in Cape Town was Alfred Milner. Milner, a contemporary of Asquith was a product of Oxford and of Balliol in a great epoch. He was a man of lofty ideas and broad progressive schemes although his bent was rather too authoritarian to fit in easily with parliamentary and democratic control. The story of his negotiations with Kruger about the position of the Uitlanders in the Transvaal is long and complicated. Fortunately in the two best general histories of this period Halévy's *History of the English People* Volume V and in Ensor's *Oxford History of England* we can see the case for or against Milner put out, Halévy against, Ensor for. They can scarcely be reconciled. Among Liberals the belief grew that Milner was a sinister figure, either bent deliberately on war or else so stiff and autocratic that he would be sure to incur the danger of war. Some however were sympathetic to him on the Liberal Imperialist side, especially some of the Oxford men, and Campbell-Bannerman was known to complain of the *religio milneriana* which afflicted many of his Oxford colleagues. When war did come at the end of 1899 it was in a manner that presented the utmost difficulties to wholehearted anti-imperialist Liberals. Britain did not invade the Transvaal. Kruger sent an ultimatum and invaded Natal and Cape Colony. Formally he seemed the aggressor and if Liberals wanted to prove that it was an unjust war they had to argue backwards showing that this and that error by Milner and others had given Kruger provocation. It was a painful task.

Campbell-Bannerman's leadership was now put to the test. His party was much divided but there was this mercy that there was no point of absolute fissure. Opinions within the party were similar to the colours of the spectrum. They shaded off from the violet of imperialism to the red of total opposition to the war. Campbell-Bannerman took up a position which may be described as left of centre. He accepted the fact of war, war declared on Britain by the Transvaal and Orange Free State in due form. He would say nothing and do nothing to hinder the efforts of British arms. He would unsay nothing of his criticisms of our pre-war policy and more and more he thought of the settlement after the war when the Boers, who must, it was agreed, be vanquished would have to have terms that would permit the two races to live together in amity. On one side were the Liberal Imperialists, with Haldane urging Liberals "to paint with a broad brush", by which he meant not to recriminate and nag the Government by harping on past events. On the other side were men like John Morley, the friend and counsellor of Gladstone, who saw the issue as a clear case of the rights of a nation against a bullying Empire.

Another figure now came to the fore. David Lloyd George, a Welshman with a deep sense of the indefeasible rights of small nations, carried his opposition to the extreme. With immense courage he announced that he would address a meeting in Birmingham itself, an almost blasphemous challenge to the authority of the great Joe. The meeting took place but no word could be uttered. A hostile audience broke it up at once and the platform party retreated to an inner room. The Chief Constable of Birmingham who had prepared for trouble, made Lloyd George dress in a police

uniform and in the midst of a large party of police he passed
through the angry mob unscathed and was quietly smuggled
out of the city.[1]

This incident, dramatic at the time, was to be of great
importance. It made Lloyd George justly a hero to the
pacifist left and when from 1916 to 1918 he had as Prime
Minister to plead for the continuation of the war to the end
against Germany it gave great strength to his arm.[2]

The Boer War fell into three phases. First there was the
overrunning of British territory and the attempts by our
armies to relieve the beleaguered towns which still held out.
This produced some severe and humiliating reverses which
shocked the country deeply. Criticism at this time had to be
stilled. Then came the advance with reinforced armies under
the celebrated general Lord Roberts, a swift advance into the
enemies' territory and a proclamation annexing both states
to the British Crown. This seemed to be the end. The Boers
were now in law British subjects; it seemed as though they
had only to be mopped up.[3]

At this point Lord Salisbury chose to ask for a dissolution
of the Parliament then five years' old. This led to what
became known as the khaki election and the popularity of the
Government, loaded as it seemed with victory, could be

[1] A cousin of the present writer who was then a young apprentice in
Birmingham and later had a successful career as an electrician in the
United States told him in Cleveland, Ohio, in 1941 that actually he and
some of his mates spotted the little Welshman with his black moustache
in the middle of the body of the police and shouted out that he was
there and that they must "get him". However in the general hubbub no
one heard them and the danger passed.

[2] It is worth recording in this connection that in Natal in 1893 a
Scottish sergeant of police saved a young Indian lawyer from lynching
by a hostile mob. His name was Ghandi, the future apostle of Indian
independence.

[3] Irish nationalism which was strongly pro-Boer took the point that
Kruger was now a British subject. It was proposed that he should be
elected for an Irish constituency to the House of Commons but nothing
came of this.

exploited. The Liberals put out the usual complaints about misuse of the prerogative of dissolution but no one paid much attention. It was not unreasonable for the Government to ask for a renewal of confidence before proceeding to a final settlement of the South African problem. The Liberals were caught at a disadvantage and they remembered with bitterness how much they suffered from the cry, "a vote for the Liberals is a vote for the Boers". It was even used against a Liberal candidate who was absent in South Africa visiting the grave of his soldier son. But in the end, for all their divisions, the Liberals did not do so badly. When the election was over the Government's majority was slightly reduced, from 152 to 134. It had indeed won another seven years of power in prospect but it was not a battle of annihilation.

And now began the unexpected and longest period of the war. The British Army had shown that it could win pitched battles against the Boers for all their admirable skill and marksmanship. But a guerrilla war was another matter. Over the vast veldt of South Africa the Boers with their splendid horsemanship and stern devotion to their cause evaded the effort of the British armies to enclose them. It became a war of cavalry, more and more horsemen were needed. What would now be done by a few aircraft had to be undertaken by battalions of horsemen. Block houses were erected, fences put up, but again and again the Boers broke through. They even surprised detachments of troops and took prisoners. General Kitchener succeeded Lord Roberts and had the hard task of ending the war. Disillusionment set in. The Boer commando leaders, the word came into our language then, became almost heroes, De Wet, de la Rey, Botha. Amongst them was a young Cambridge graduate Smuts, later Field Marshal, Privy Councillor and Chancellor of Cambridge University. Contingents from Australia, New Zealand and Canada, nations most apt for this equestrian warfare were sent. But in the eyes of the world the British Empire came to present a sorry spectacle. In Europe and America opinion was deeply against us. We were always odious; we now became ridiculous. To hasten the war Kitchener resolved on a practice which might be justified by dire necessity but which doubled the load of odium we had to bear. The farmhouses of the Boers while they stood were continual sources of supply and reinforcement. Kitchener ordered their evacuation and destruction and the non-combatants, women and children, were taken to concentration camps hurriedly erected by the army. They were said to be well cared for and well provided but soon it was known that many of the inmates were dying of disease.[1] General Hertzog, a future Nationalist Prime Minister of the Union of South Africa, lost several of his children in these camps. It was later complained here that he was very "sour" towards Britain.

At this point Campbell-Bannerman made a decisive move. In a speech he denounced the use of the concentration camps as "methods of barbarism". He was bitterly denounced as a denigrator of gallant British fighting men. In vain did he explain that it was the method and not the agents which he was censuring. But the phrase went deep. It appealed to a feeling of humanity. Many of his colleagues were dismayed by his imprudence but deep in the broad, radical stratum of the party there was admiration and gratitude; they knew themselves to be led by a man of humanity, principle and courage. When in 1902 the Boer leaders came to a conference and negotiated with Milner and Kitchener a treaty by which the fighting ended there was deep satisfaction in Britain. But underneath there were doubts and anxieties. What was wrong with our military system that so small a nation should require for its defeat a force of active males outnumbering their entire population? What was wrong with our colonial and foreign policy that we seemed to be without a friend in

[1] Professor J. S. Haldane of Oxford, brother of the statesman and a gifted physiologist, was able to visit the camps. On return he expressed the opinion that much of the disease was due to the excessive rations of beef, fat and flour with little vegetable.

the world? Outwardly all was patriotic rejoicing. The troops came home with colours flying, war memorials were erected: strangely out of scale they seemed later when more terrible wars had to be commemorated. But the public had had a severe shock. The pacification of South Africa and the reform of the army had to be faced. We shall see how this was the task of the next Liberal Government.

In justice to the Conservative administration, now under the Prime Ministership of the gifted Arthur Balfour who succeeded Lord Salisbury in 1902, a prompt effort was made to deal with the diplomatic isolation of Britain. His foreign secretary, Lord Lansdowne, began a slow and patient effort to find friends on the continent. With the approval and help of King Edward VII he made approaches to France and began the policy which became known as the Entente Cordiale. It was not an alliance but an understanding. All the sore spots of abrasion between France and Britain, in Africa, Indo-China, the Pacific and elsewhere were made subject to friendly agreement. France, in constant danger from Germany, was led to expect British aid in the event of attack but no promise was given. This was in the main a non-party matter. Liberals welcomed any relaxation of tension. They claimed to be the party of peace; they could not oppose this important step to peace. There were doubters, including Lord Rosebery himself, now retired from active politics but still influential. He foreboded that the agreement with France would in effect align us inevitably against Germany. With him, although not very vocal, were some of the younger and more radical members of the party, the future Labour M.P. and Peer, Arthur Ponsonby and W. H. Hirst the Editor of the *Economist*. This doubting and suspicious element was of importance later on when the choice between neutrality and fighting with France had to be made. It was perhaps even more important retrospectively after 1918 when swords were sheathed and pens filled and our foreign policy examined. The virulent francophobia of the

British Left in the nineteen twenties drew much encouragement from the anti-entente Liberals. When Lord Rosebery died in 1929 he received a commendation in the *New Statesman* for his foresight.

The period from 1902 to 1906 was one of good hope for the Liberals. They confronted a powerful administration with Balfour and for a time Chamberlain. Balfour was a man of acute and subtle mind, a wealthy Scottish Laird but allied by blood to the great House of Cecil; he was the nephew of Lord Salisbury. He was a distinguished figure in the Tory social world and underneath an apparently mild exterior a man of tenacious convictions. Chamberlain, a power in himself, represented the new forces of Liberal Unionism now merging very tightly with Conservatism. Against them the Liberals could field a strong team. Asquith, a lawyer of pluperfect competence, Grey, Haldane, Bryce, Morley, the famous dockers' leader John Burns, rising young intellectuals like the future minister and famous banker Reginald McKenna; Herbert Gladstone represented his father's famous name. Yet they had a long way to go. If they could pull the Government's majority down to 130 this was only with the aid of 80 Irish. It would need no ordinary swing of the pendulum to put them securely in power.

In the last three years of that Parliament controversial and popular issues fell into the Liberals' lap like ripe plums. The Balfour Government, though short and internally troubled, was efficient. It had many good things to its credit. Yet it was its fate that whether its actions were good or ill they became unpopular and gave ammunition to the enemy. At home they embarked on a revision of the system of education. In many ways our present educational structure was cast by this Bill. But almost everything about it offended Liberal susceptibilities. Wisely no doubt it merged secondary with elementary education and removed the school boards set up by Forster's Act of 1870. But the Liberals loved the school boards and were proud of them and Liberals have always a bias in favour of any formal democracy. The transfer to Counties and County Boroughs with coopted members seemed a Tory trick. Still more alarming was the provision for putting Church schools on the rates instead of central grants. The Act was avowedly devised to save the Church schools. Gladstone had mortgaged his popularity with the dissenters by his tenderness to Church schools in 1870. He had first met the young radical Joseph Chamberlain on this issue. And now the elderly Joe was sitting passively in the Cabinet which was making matters so much worse. Liberal odium against him mounted. This education issue was important but must be regarded as what we may call a factional issue. The public in general were not deeply stirred, but dissenting opinion was. The opposition was bitter and long and when the act came into force dissenters, especially in Wales, refused to pay rates and went to prison. It was not an issue on which to convert people but it was the kind of issue which animated supporters, brought out cheque books and canvassers. On Ireland the Balfour Ministry took what they thought might be the last step in the policy of killing Home Rule with kindness. The Chief Secretary, Wyndham, carried an Act which made it possible for large parts of the soil of Ireland to be purchased by the tenants. Liberals could not blame them for this. They had themselves moved towards purchase in 1886. But the effect was spoiled when later Wyndham had to resign because his permanent secretary had seemed to encourage a proposal for a council which, faint though it was, seemed to lean towards Home Rule. This victory for extreme unionist opinion confirmed Liberals in their belief that Conservatives could never conciliate.

A useful licensing act provided for the reduction of public houses, a policy dear to the Liberals, but as they could not approve of the compensation offered to the wicked publicans temperance opinion was roused. This was another factional issue. The mass of the people were not inclined to welcome restraints and the Conservatives could play on this. As

5*

Halévy has put it: "The old Tory party, which viewed with an indulgent eye the coarse pleasures that helped the lower classes to endure their poverty cheerfully, had for many years found it good electioneering-tactics to oppose the puritanism of the radicals on this point". (Vol. V, p. 380.) But once again the zealots were animated on the Liberal side.

It only remained for an issue to arise which would make a broad general appeal, which could be preached far and wide to all and sundry, which would deliver the Liberals from their middle class cantonment. And two such issues did arise. One concerned the Trades Unions which both parties had learned by bitter experience to regard with deep electoral respect. The Taff Vale Judgement of 1901, and other decisions by the Law Courts put so restrictive an interpretation on the Act of 1875 which had been regarded as the Unions' charter that Unions now felt that the strike weapon was taken from them. The kernel of the matter was that Unions, like all other associations, were to be liable for the torts, the wrong-doing, of the members and so might be faced with pleas for damage which would be crippling. Both the two parties were very much dependent on and composed of manufacturers and other employers, but the tilt of the Liberals towards modified socialistic legislation gave them a chance of promising more. The Government did not act with decision and when the dissolution occurred the wrath of the workers fell on them.

But one more issue was wanted, one which would combine worker and master, poor and rich, one that would challenge the most firmly held assumptions and most pious myths of nineteenth century economics. It was forthcoming. And strangest of all it was provided by the Arch-enemy, the hated Joe Chamberlain himself. On returning from a tour in Africa he began to advocate an economic Union of the Empire. This would imply tariffs on goods from foreign countries. He had a formidable array of arguments, for British manu-facturing industry had to face competition more severe than in the time of Bright and Cobden; Germany and the United States were the countries most frequently mentioned. Birmingham, the hardware town, had industries which were threatened. The Cotton industry of Lancashire was also under stress and while Manchester was the classical capital of Free Trade it was never so securely radical as the West Riding. The plea for protection of manufacturing interests, right or wrong, was simple and intelligible. But when this was coupled with the idea of Empire Free Trade he was faced with the awkward fact that the dominions and colonies were mainly exporters of primary products, raw materials, and any scheme that would satisfy them must impose a tariff on the non-empire imports. Logically this meant a tax on food. He thus placed the Conservatives in a very awkward position. Were they to go back to the dark days before Peel and tax the people's food? This dilemma they never succeeded in solving and even by 1914 they were still in two minds about it. But Chamberlain's plunge into protectionism (he called it Tariff Reform to avert the evil eye), at once weakened the Cabinet. Chamberlain resigned and the Duke of Devonshire and some Free Traders resigned also. It was a weakened Cabinet that carried on the government. The Liberals hailed this all with unalloyed delight. What could be better to unite the party and to bring it new support than to fight the old free trade battle once again, an argument in which they knew all the answers and had a perfect armoury of weapons? The whole phalanx of academic economists was with them. The sophisticated modern economist reviewing their arguments now might think them over-simple and abstract. But for several generations educated and thinking British citizens had learned the case for free trade and could not be shaken. It gave the Liberals an ideal issue on which to fight.

It is part of the technique of British politics that the Conservative party to keep in power must give itself the airs of a moderately progressive party. There must always be a

Tamworth manifesto look about it. It must always have an element that may claim to be more forward than many radicals, a Disraeli, a Lord Randolph Churchill or a Butler. Equally it is a technique of the radicals that they must be able to unmask these pretensions; they must be able to prove that the Tories are Tories still, that they are not only stick-in-the-mud but positively "reactionary". Behind the mask of a Canning you must discover an Eldon, behind a Peel a Lyndhurst or Lord George Bentinck. And now they could play such a card and persuade the people that the old protectionist slogans which had been used to shore up Tory protectionism in the hungry forties were being bandied about once more. Liberals began to enjoy not a dispersion but a concentration of their forces. The older war horses reared their heads and prepared for battle; the younger men who might lean to socialism or military imperialism or both could be harnessed to more pacific and less dangerous tasks. All good men might come to the aid of the party.

For two years there took place a remarkable public debate. It was carried on in the press, select and popular, and by hundreds of orators. But the centre of the contest was a series of speeches by Chamberlain in town after town, and answers by Asquith who was now recognised as incomparably the best debater and the clearest expositor of the Liberal faith. From the complexity of issues which were moving opinion at this time it is not possible to measure the extent to which Free Trade won votes, but few people doubted that it was, certain places and industries excepted, a favourable issue for the Liberals. They had now received almost every electoral boon for which they might have hoped, when Providence in its bounty gave them still one more.

One of the arguments of the extreme pro-Boer Liberals had been that the mainspring of the imperialist desire to occupy the Transvaal had been the need to secure the wealthy gold mines of the Rand. According to this line of thought the war had been in the plainest and most brutal sense "a capitalists' war". As a diagnosis of the designs and dreams of our imperialists this accusation was narrow and unfair. But the interests of the mineowners of the Rand and their thousands of shareholders in this country were a very obvious material interest which counted with the others. It was even maintained, on one occasion by a Conservative Member in the House, that since the war resulted in the occupation of Johannesburg, the gold industry, as the beneficiaries, should be made to pay for the war. This cry was naturally heard on the extreme Left also. Lloyd George had nicknamed the mine magnates "Randlords" and the pun had been well received. But the ideas of making the randlords pay were simple-minded and absurd. The effects of the war were to make great difficulties for the industry especially labour difficulties. The menial work was usually carried out by black labour and after the war for various reasons it was in short supply. The mines were in great difficulty, their capital outlay was immense; there were other gold-fields in the world. Labour they must have and that quickly. The Government after rather hasty consideration approved of an ingenious scheme to import Chinese labourers. These men were to be indentured for a period of years; they were to receive reasonable pay and be kept and disciplined in their own compounds and to a starving coolie in Canton it was not a bad proposition. But the project caused a tremendous outcry. The Boers objected strongly and by this time the Boers were regarded by the Liberals as their friends, the objects of their high-minded patronage. Opinion in this country was quite genuinely shocked; on humanitarian grounds, for the scheme seemed to savour of slavery, however carefully it was distinguished by the careful system of "indenture". Men were to be called from afar, shut up in a compound and put to work. It was to be one vast workhouse, one Bastille, peopled by dangerous and sinister orientals. It should be remembered that the dangerous Boxer rebellion in China repressed by the European powers had taken place only in 1900 and was fresh in people's minds. The Liberals on the "Chinese Slavery issue", as it was called, had a very good case for argument. They had something much better, a threat to white employment generally, for what was done in one part of the Empire might be done elsewhere, and also an upsurge of crude xenophobia, hatred of the alien, the yellow devil. It was by all accounts a big factor in the election of 1906. To the Conservatives it was regarded as the supreme electoral atrocity, cancelling out any khaki elections past or to come. The memory of this bitter defeat and what they regarded as the dishonest and unscrupulous use of the term "slavery" by respectable politicians lingered long. It was a factor in the bitter and desperate opposition they were to offer to Asquith some years later.

And now all was ready for the battle. The Liberals had been winning by-elections handsomely for some time. The end came quicker than was expected. At the beginning of December 1906 Balfour encouraged, it is thought, by some signs of a revival of dispute between the imperialist and anti-imperialist sections of the Liberal party, decided to resign, and catch them off their guard. The King sent for Sir Henry Campbell-Bannerman to form an administration. He did so. Not without some personal difficulties because of an effort by Asquith, Haldane and Grey to send Campbell-Bannerman to the Lords and leave Asquith supreme in the Commons. In lives of Asquith and others this "plot" as it was called has been fully described. In the end Campbell-Bannerman came out with enhanced authority. The dissolution had to be postponed till after Christmas and the polling extending over ten days was complete by the end of January. The result was a Liberal victory that surprised all observers, the new Prime Minister perhaps having been the most justly optimistic. The main feature of the election was the sweeping of all the characteristically radical areas by the Liberals and the Labour candidates working in an agreed alliance with them. The usual Tory stronghold in southern England was invaded and many unexpected seats fell in the Home Counties. When the fight was over the Liberals and their allies had a majority of 358 over the number of 156 Conservatives and Unionists. This was the lowest the Conservatives had fallen since the election of 1833 that followed the Reform Bill. The Liberal majority was such that it left them free of Irish support and even free of support by the fifty Labour members now returned. The new members thronged into Westminster full of eager dreams and plans. Who they were and what they were to do is the subject of our next chapter.[1]

---

[1] In referring to the date of the Campbell-Bannerman-Asquith Ministry there is usually some confusion. The Ministry dates from 4th December 1905 when Sir Henry kissed hands. The election was in January 1906 and the history of the Ministry seems to start from that point. But the appointment of a ministry is one thing; the election of a Parliament is another and the distinction should be observed. From early December Campbell-Bannerman was governing the country. Before the election was over he had to deal with a dangerous crisis in foreign affairs threatening war with Germany, in which he took decisive and memorable action. Election or no election the King's Government must be carried on and full responsibility rests on those who have accepted ministerial office.

SEVEN

THE LIBERAL MINISTRY

THE MINISTRY which Campbell-Bannerman formed in December 1905 is justly remembered as one of the most distinguished which has taken office. It may be considered as one continuous Liberal Ministry from its formation until May 1915 when a coalition government of all parties was formed still under Asquith. Formally there was a change in April 1908 when Campbell-Bannerman retired shortly before his death and Asquith succeeded by universal consent. When a Prime Minister retires for personal reasons and someone of the same party succeeds it is a convention of the Constitution that all his colleagues are deemed to have resigned with him and all the offices are free for the new Prime Minister to dispose of. In such cases there is a considerable rearrangement of the Ministry, some figures depart and others are brought in and promoted but there is no sharp break in the continuity of the Administration. This is quite different from a resignation of a Prime Minister brought about by a defeat in the House of Commons as in 1885 or 1895 or 1924, or defeat in a general election as in 1874, 1880, 1892, 1922, 1929, 1945 and 1951. A ministry may break up because of internal dissent as in 1916, 1940 or 1945, before the general election of that year. Thinking in terms of political reality we consider a party administration to have lasted during the period when that party has had continuous support from the majority of the House of Commons. Thus we speak of the Conservative Ministry of 1895 to 1905 although there were two Prime Ministers, Salisbury and Balfour and one general election in 1900. The Liberal Ministry of 1905 saw one change of Prime Minister and three elections, the election of 1906 which confirmed it in power and the two elections of January and December 1910 which enabled it to remain securely in power although its majority was to depend on 40 Labour members and 80 Irish Nationalists.

We may therefore take the period from 1906 to the opening of the war in 1914 as a whole, considerable as the changes in individual ministers were and different as the issues and the temper of politics were to become during this time.

While the leader, Campbell-Bannerman, was of pure Gladstonian vintage and a hero to the Radicals, many of the principal offices went to those who were considered Liberal Imperialists, such as Asquith at the Exchequer, Grey at the Foreign Office, and Haldane whom Campbell-Bannerman distrusted and sent somewhat disdainfully to the War Office. An eminent but never striking figure was Lord Crewe, a quiet and competent patrician statesman undeviatingly Liberal but a force for moderation and agreement. He held various important offices and from 1908 led the Liberal Party in the House of Lords. Senior Gladstonians, considered as generally anti-imperialist, were Lord Loreburn, Sir Robert Reid, who was Lord Chancellor till 1912, James Bryce, afterwards Viscount Bryce who was Secretary for Ireland until sent to Washington as Ambassador and John Morley, afterwards Viscount Morley, who rather to his disgust was given the Secretaryship of State for India. As these senior men passed on or out of office the younger Liberal Imperialist school appeared to become more dominating. It was however mainly in appearance. The radicals at first seemed to be of little importance. John Burns the former workers' leader was given the Local Government Board at which later he was to pass the first Town-Planning Act. But with the advent of Lloyd George to Cabinet office as President of the Board of Trade the radical element won such influence in the ministry that when in 1908 Asquith was constrained to make him Chancellor of the Exchequer his effective political power became equal almost to that of Asquith himself. He was, as it were, the young Joe Chamberlain of the ministry. In spite of his lack of a formal university education, possibly indeed because of it, he had an eager, thrusting, creative mind, always seeking for new political devices, seeing social and political problems with a fresh mind unclouded by the polite scepticism which his colleagues had acquired by their education and professional training. We must not be blinded by the retrospective knowledge that he and Asquith were to break into open and bitter enmity. While they worked in harness they brought to the leadership of British government a combination of intellectual powers such as has rarely been equalled. There was one other member of the ministry, not in Cabinet office until 1908, and that was young Winston Churchill, the son of Lord Randolph who had been such an intolerable gadfly to Liberals in the eighteen eighties. By his original training he was a soldier but he had also been press-correspondent and author and his life of his father at an early age had won him the respect of political historians. In the earlier days of the ministry he was regarded as a radical and his name, strange as it may now seem, was linked with that of Lloyd George in opposing military and advocating social service expenditure. When in 1912 he became First Lord of the Admiralty that phase of his career ended. His genius, in General de Gaulle's words, "apt for all things pertaining to the study and conduct of war", was given its chance to develop. He was at all times a profoundly unpopular member of the Cabinet. He had "ratted" from the Conservative party with some other younger men on the Free Trade issue. Conservative dislike of the Ministry which, starting slowly, was to rise by 1914 almost into frenzy, found it natural to execrate beyond all others the man who had not only betrayed his party but betrayed his father's political legacy.

The new House of Commons which assembled at the end of January 1906 presented a remarkable spectacle. For one thing, of the 670 members as many as 310 were new members. This is most unusual. Indeed there had never been so complete a turnover since the Revolution. Our parliamentary life works on the assumption that it must be continuous. It is like one of these fabulous Christmas puddings which are said to have been stirred by Queen Elizabeth the First, a portion being left to form the basis of next year's pudding. Both in respect of experience of government in general and of parliamentary procedure we count on a large element of any one House to take over in the new House and to teach the newcomers the rules. Victorian Parliaments saw much less violent changes in personnel and in the period before the second Reform Bill it was common enough for something like two fifths of the seats to be uncontested. But now the Liberal members numbering 380 included 220 who were there for the first time. However if there is a reasonably large leaven of experienced members the House will work well enough. But the presence of so many new men, many of them young, coming in on what seemed a tidal wave of radical victory tended to spread an apocalyptic spirit and a desire to make all things new. When the first few years of the Parliament passed in relative quiescence and inadequate performance, which could be blamed on the Lords or the general cursedness of human things, there was a reversion into disillusion which was to be damaging to the Liberal cause.

The new Parliament was young and fresh and radical. It had another interesting feature. It was the least Anglican House of Commons there had been since before the Restoration. It was reckoned that 180 members of the new House were Protestant Dissenters and when Roman Catholics and Jews were counted, the habitual Anglican dominance was reduced to a majority of about forty. Naturally the victors assumed that the "infamous" Education Act of 1902 would be repealed and reversed. But a tally of religious origins and affiliations may not represent the whole truth. In many individual cases not only the sectarian attachment but the religious faith was weakening. Just as many of the formally Anglican members would appear as faint and feeble in their religion to an Anglican zealot like Lord Hugh Cecil, so many of the formally nonconformist members would be somewhat agnostic in their outlook and their support of nonconformist measures more a matter of loyalty than of deep conviction. English radicalism, including in that term both Liberals and Socialists, always contained an element of definitely non-religious men who as a matter of intellectual honesty would not call themselves members of any Christian church. Many nominal Anglicans no doubt were equally feeble in the faith but were less likely to proclaim it. The mass-gravitation towards the greater Anglican orb remained, theirs were the noble fanes and ancient village churches, the chapels of colleges, the famous schools staffed with zealous chaplains, the great benefices of the Church to endow and attract gifted men of religious leanings, the solemn services of baptism, matrimony and sepulture, administered to and for the great majority of wealthy, eminent and educated Englishmen in proportion as they were educated, eminent and wealthy, and the sacred rite of the Coronation and consecration of the Sovereign, "in all causes ecclesiastical as well as temporal within this kingdom supreme". And since in England religious attachment could never be separated from class it may be noted that the new House contained fewer rich men and more poorer professional men and others. A sign of this was that with little delay the new House altered the time of rising at the end of a sitting from 12.0 o'clock to 11.0 o'clock in order that the less affluent members might return home more cheaply by public transport.

If the triumph of nonconformity and the more old-fashioned Liberal ideas was less strong than it might seem in outward appearance, there was one respect in which Liberals might clearly see a threat to their continued ascendancy. The Victory of 1906 was not entirely an effort of Liberalism proper. It was to some extent an alliance between the new Labour Party and the main body of Liberals. Labour members had appeared in Parliament before, notably the famous Keir Hardie, the originator and prophet of the Independent Labour Party. In 1903 a Labour candidate, Will Crooks, had won a sensational victory over a Unionist candidate, the Liberals not intervening. For the election of 1906 about 50 Labour candidates were sponsored by the Trades Union Council including some generally regarded as Liberal. A more purely political body, the Labour Representation Committee, endorsed the candidature of some but not all of these. The election resulted in 29 of the Labour Representation candidates being returned. This was a body sworn to political independence of other parties and in addition there were about twenty members of Labour and working class complexion who would sympathise with them although generally classed by the term Lib.-Lab. But even the Labour members sworn to independence had not been in reality independent in their election. A pact had been agreed upon between Herbert Gladstone and Ramsay MacDonald, the Labour leader, to prevent Labour and Liberals damaging each other's chances by presenting rival candidates. The immediate need was to defeat the Tories and Unionists. None the less the appearance of the new element in Parliament, socialistic, consciously proletarian, different in doctrine and in social texture from the orthodox middle class Liberal, was significant. With gleeful malice, not untinged with fear, the Conservative commentators pointed out this "writing on the wall" this presaged doom of the so-called People's Party that had played the democrat and must now see their power pass to people whose democracy was much more real and more terrible. This was the cloud no larger than a man's hand which would soon overspread the sky. The more thoughtful Liberals realised the truth of much of this diagnosis and in the next decade anxiously discussed measures by which they might keep their hold over the working class masses who had not always supported them but without whose support they must cease to exist as a major party.

But the imminence of Labour superiority at this time must not be exaggerated. The elections of 1910 brought them no greater numbers; the Labour strength was reckoned at 40 only. The fact was that the two parties shared many causes, free trade, peace and dislike of armaments, in varying degrees anti-imperialism and hostility to the Church interest and to the House of Lords. Both by their general doctrine were inclined to favour reasonable autonomy for Ireland and the South African Colonies. Except in a few constituencies, mostly mining constituencies, the Labour candidates had little chance of success unless the Liberal candidate stood aside and in many constituencies the Liberals depended on a similar abstinence by Labour. At any time it was within the power of the Liberals by refusing to make some accommodation with Labour to sweep the party out of Parliament. They were sorely tempted, goaded and derided as they often were for being capitalist lackeys, wolves in sheep's clothing, no less bourgeois and reactionary than the Conservatives. Two factors restrained the Liberal leadership from such a move. One was immediate and practical; they would make a Conservative victory almost certain, for Labour could take away at least as many seats from them as they could from Labour. Deeper down was a more ethical and far-reaching consideration. Liberals sincerely believed in democracy, they believed that the majority of the people should in the long run have the chance to work its will. Their task was to make the people see the Liberals as their true friends, as the authentic spearhead of progress. The path of right conduct as well as of prudence was to persevere against all discouragements in the way of friendship and alliance rather than to precipitate an open break. The socialist zealot might genuinely see the alternative between Liberal and Tory government as a fine shade of difference and care little which he suffered from. The Liberals looked with genuine fear and distaste to a period of Unionist rule under men whose influence was clearly dangerous and baneful, Chamberlain, Balfour, Milner, Carson, Curzon. Fundamentally there was a deep disagreement between Liberal and Labour as to what politics was about. Was it about wealth, its distribution and ownership? Or was it about government, about the rights of men and of nations, the policies of states and Empires? Was there such a thing as a political issue, a matter of faith and principle? Or were such issues only reflections of a greater *economic* reality? The question is still in dispute.

One matter of the first importance was settled quickly and finally by Campbell-Bannerman and by him personally. The Unionist Government had settled terms of peace in South Africa on distinctly generous terms. They had offered grants for the reconstruction of the devastated farms and in the Transvaal and the Orange Free State, formerly independent republics but now Colonies of the Crown, they had set to work with zeal and skill in the task of reconstruction. This was the work for which Milner was most suited and his assistants, a number of able and rather idealistic young men who were known as "Milner's kindergarten", many of whom lived to be elder statesmen of a somewhat dispirited imperialism, did much excellent work. But the major problem was how these provinces were to be governed. Milner's successor as High Commissioner for South Africa, Lord Selborne, had set up Councils with representation for the Boers. With this many, even some Liberals, were satisfied. Conquered peoples are not often treated so generously. What few fully realised was that there had been a conquest and that that was the supreme fact to the Boers. The exact terms of their subjugation were a minor matter. The English are an imperial people. It has been perhaps a misfortune that in modern times they have known so little of defeat. This narrows the sphere of their political experience and stunts their political imagination. Since the Dutch wars of Charles II

Englishmen had known no defeat, with one exception. That was the defeat in the War of American Independence but that could be attributed to the action of men of their own race and the misguided policy of George III and his ministers. It has always come as a surprise that their defeated enemies should "live so much in the past" should be unable to forget old resentments. The bitterness of eating bread that is only the bounty of a victor is unknown to them.

Liberal principles, the principles of Fox and Durham and Gladstone demanded that subjects of the Crown, being European and Christian, should not be expected to live in political subjection. The logic of Liberalism demanded that the Boers should be permitted to govern themselves. However it is not often that the logic of a political principle is fully acted upon. It is the claim to greatness of Campbell-Bannerman that he for once acted on the full logic of his principles. He proposed, to the anxiety of many of his more cautious colleagues, that it was necessary to give the people of the Transvaal full representative and responsible government such as was enjoyed by the white dominions of the Crown. Lloyd George has testified that Campbell-Bannerman's fifteen minutes' speech in which he persuaded the Cabinet to this course was the most impressive intellectual performance he had ever witnessed. The essence of the proposal was that the Government should be "responsible", that not only could the people elect a Parliament but that that Parliament should be able to designate a leader who would be first minister and hold the effective executive power. This was done without the process of long debate over a Bill since it was a prerogative matter and could be settled by Letters Patent. In July 1906 the Government decision was announced. A wide franchise for whites, no official non-elected members, full control of their own affairs. General Botha, one of the most eminent of the Boer leaders, became Prime Minister of the Transvaal and in 1907 he was attending an Imperial Conference in London and became very much the popular attraction amongst the visiting ministers: Austen Chamberlain wrote rather disgustedly to his father that while the Boers were no doubt good fellows he was becoming tired of the continual adulation of them to the neglect of the other colonies and dominions who after all had fought on our side.

The bold step of enfranchising the Boers was followed in a few years' time by the Union of the four colonies which made up British South Africa into a Union which at once became a Dominion equal in status and comparable in wealth to Canada and Australia.

What were the benefits of this policy which Conservatives denounced as dangerous and foolish? It has stood up to terrible tests. For fifty years the Union survived and in spite of the rancour of a large part of the Boer population the Union acted with Great Britain in the two great wars and South African divisions contributed to the total British strength. In the Union there was, with one exception, internal peace and the country prospered and flourished. Ten, perhaps even five years ago, most people and all Liberals would have generally agreed that this was indeed a triumph of Whig-Liberal thought and an illustration of how trust and cooperation are better than repressive authority. Now we are wondering about it. South Africa has left the Commonwealth and declared itself a Republic thus satisfying the patriotic sentiments of the Afrikaners and distressing the English citizens in the Union. But behind this movement is a greater problem, the treatment of the coloured population. Nowhere does the South African policy of *apartheid* call forth more condemnation than amongst present day Liberals. And it must be admitted that the problem was visible in 1906. It was quite clear to the informed members of the Liberal Government that the Boers had no intention, however gradually, of emancipating the natives and trying to find some way in which they might slowly become citizens in any degree equal to the whites. And now people are heard to say

that Milner was right and Campbell-Bannerman wrong.
What are we to make of this?

It will no doubt become an almost classic, text-book
question on political prudence and justice. The settlement of
1906 did ignore the native problem. The problem that faced
the Liberal Government was whether to risk a settlement of
the old dispute between Dutch and British settlers by keeping
in the forefront the native question. To safeguard the natives
it would be necessary to lay some important restraints upon
the power of the elective parliaments that were to be set up.
To do that would make it impossible to get the free assent of
the Boers. Campbell-Bannerman took the course of making
peace with those whose assent was essential to peace. The
native problem, with many heart searchings, was left to the
future; it was an act of faith, the avoidance of the greatest and
most immediate evil in the hope that in time the other question might become easier. This was the easier for Liberals to
do for their inherent "meliorism", their belief in some kind of
natural progress, encouraged a vague hope that men and
things would improve. These hopes have not been fulfilled.
But before passing judgment it is necessary to consider what
was possible and probable in the circumstances of South
African politics. We may say that if Milner and men like him
could have ruled South Africa justly with consideration for
all elements, British, Boer and Kaffir, this would have been
best. But this is to suppose that the British Government had
the power and the will to sustain in South Africa the force
necessary to carry out the will of the imperial government.
At much expense and in time of peace it might have done so.
But war came. In 1914 a section of the Boers rebelled under
former generals De Wet and de la Rey. They were suppressed by Botha and troops who remained loyal to the
settlement of the Union. Without the full Liberal concessions
it may be considered certain that Botha and the entire Dutch
population would have taken the chance to rise and drive the
British to the sea and little help could have come when all

forces were being mobilised for war in France. What we would then have seen would have been not Milner's wise British autocracy but a Boer Republic supported by and allied to a probably victorious Imperial Germany.

Whatever the long run verdict may be, the fact of the settlement of 1906 and its gratifying sequel in the Union gave much prestige to the Liberal Government. In the English-speaking world outside Britain it tended to strengthen the principle of autonomy and Home Rule and to make opinion favourable to the attempt to give Home Rule to Ireland. But within the United Kingdom opinion on this vexed question had hardened so much that it was doubtful if the Liberals gained more than a talking point from their South African triumph.

Another nettle was firmly grasped by Campbell-Bannerman. One of the first obligations of the new Government was to amend the law relating to Trades Unions in the conduct of strikes. Strong support had come to them from the workers' organisations in the belief that they would remove the disabilities under which the Unions suffered since the famous Taff Vale judgment in the law courts had interpreted the law so strictly against the unions. A Royal Commission had reported just after the election and in the light of this report the government lawyers prepared a Bill designed to satisfy the workers' demands in terms satisfactory to jurists. But its legalistic terms, reinterpreting "the law of agency", were obscure and unsatisfactory to the Radicals. A few days later a Labour Bill was presented enacting in simple terms that a trade union could never be made liable for damages on account of the illegal acts of its members. Campbell-Bannerman intervened to say that he preferred the clear and simple terms of the Labour Bill and would accept them on behalf of the Government. To the private dismay of some of his legal colleagues this was done and before the session was over the Trades Disputes Act of 1906 became law. It was an important victory for the Radicals. The Conservative opposition

were half-hearted and the Bill was let through by the Lords
as a matter of political prudence. Lawyers disapproved and
many Liberals were uneasy in their mind, for by this Act
Trades Unions secured a privileged position that no other
association enjoyed. Theoretically it was wrong: in practice
it might be justified by accepting the thesis that Trades
Unions by their peculiar needs and tasks were different from
other associations and required some special dispensation.
When between 1911 and 1914 there arose a series of alarming
strikes and labour disputes it was held against the Liberals
that they had by their frightened demagogy put the order
and prosperity of the nation in danger. Business men and
industrial leaders tended more and more to weaken in
allegiance and transfer to the Conservatives. But politically
it had the merits of the clean-cut, a definite and simple
reform and the Prime Minister won, in this and other ways,
the affection and respect of the radical elements that his
successor Asquith could never attain. Another instalment of
"social reform" was granted in 1906 in the form of a Work-
men's Compensation Act which enlarged the number of those
who could claim compensation from accident or various
forms of illness contracted in their employment. The last acts
on this subject had been passed by the Unionists in 1897 and
1900: the new act was much more radical and was estimated
to raise the number of workers covered from seven million
to thirteen.

The year 1906 therefore saw a radical Parliament acting
radically in the impulse of the great electoral victory. The
next two years were a period of disappointment. It was
necessary to satisfy the aspirations of some of those sections
of the party who had particular grievances to redress such as
the nonconformists offended by the pro-Anglican Act of
1902 and the Temperance section anxious for more effective
restraints on drink. These however were sectional interests.
To say this is not in any way to condemn the policies
advocated for which there was a good case, but to emphasise

that they were not matters of very wide public concern amongst the electorate as a whole. The Opposition realised that on these issues, unlike the Trades Unions issue, they could fight, and a Licencing Bill was rejected by the Lords who also prevented any progress on the Education question. A Bill to abolish plural voting was also rejected in the Upper House and some smaller measures such as a Small-holders Bill for Scotland foundered also. Liberal anger mounted steadily but not general anger among the public. The Conservative strategy at this point was well calculated.

But more important in the end than all these domestic questions was the question of defence. One part of this concerned the Army which the new Secretary of State for War, Haldane, set out scientifically to reform. Much study had been done since the failures of the Boer War and Haldane now set out to provide a better organisation at the top. Some of this had been begun by Balfour who had set up the Committee of Imperial Defence a body of military advisers sitting with the Cabinet Ministers most concerned. Haldane added an effective General Staff for the Army and made preparations for swift and effective mobilisation which would provide six divisions ready for service on the Continent on the outbreak of war. The old volunteer units and yeomanry were made into a new Territorial Army charged with home defence. All this was done without an increase in the estimates. Haldane encountered opposition in the House and elsewhere but he had the confidence of the leading officers and on the whole succeeded in his plan without creating any political storm.

Much more dangerous and difficult was the question of the Navy. From the beginning of the century and more evidently from 1906 onwards it became clear that Britain was facing a deliberate and calculated challenge to its naval supremacy that it had not faced since 1860 when Louis Napoleon seemed to have dangerous designs. This challenge came from the German Empire. It was a strange duel, between two nations habitually friendly in the past, between two sovereigns, Uncle and Nephew, Edward VII and Kaiser Wilhelm II, and between two great seamen and naval planners, Admiral Fisher in England and Admiral Tirpitz the German Navy minister in Berlin. These two men are probably the two greatest Admirals in naval history who were never fated to command fleets in action.

No responsible Government of Great Britain could contemplate sacrificing supremacy at sea. If the Liberal party always harboured some pure pacifists, they could never prevail to this extent. But they could dispute about the margin of superiority we should maintain. For a long time past it had been the two-power standard, that is, a navy equal to the two next greatest. This was now in danger. Germany with its great industrial and scientific resources and its purposeful military government was in process of narrowing the margin. Admiral Fisher however had in a sense brilliantly stolen a march on all other navies by his creation of the new Dreadnought type of battleship, larger, swifter, and more powerfully armed to the extent that it had more power in long-range guns than any two of the existing battleships. This had dangers, for if it rendered the battleships of other navies obsolete it did the same to our own. Against this Fisher and his First Lord of Admiralty, Lord Cawdor, had provided for a pace of construction of the new ships that would leave other navies far behind and, if it was fully carried out, emphasise British supremacy. The Liberal Government when it took office had to take a decision whether to carry on with this programme or relax it. It was in the nature of Liberal thought and sentiment that it put a presumption in favour of relaxation. This would have been so at any time, but in 1907 a Peace Conference of the Powers was to assemble at The Hague to discuss possible schemes of disarmament. This was dear to the Liberal heart; it was in accordance with Gladstonian ideals, concert of civilised governments striving for the peace of all. The Government decided to reduce the Cawdor construction programme. If The Hague Conference failed, and it did fail, then construction could be speeded up. But meanwhile Tirpitz had been given his chance to creep up. By 1909 the British public was seriously alarmed; the Liberals were losing by-elections mainly it is thought on the naval issue. The public in these days was conscious of naval affairs to an extent not imaginable now.

Every schoolboy then at a moment's notice could draw a rough plan of a Dreadnought or pre-Dreadnought ship with its armament. Many other matters were technical and obscure, the need for better docks in different places, the use of torpedoes, the penetrating power of shells. But everyone could see and measure the number of capital ships available to each power. A government that weakened on that issue was an unpopular government. The force of pacific opinion was strong but it had definite limits, there was little chance that it could expand into new social and political strata. It was more or less a fixed dimension. But the pride, the care, the anxiety of the nation for the Navy was an illimitable force. It is probably a fair judgment to say that while in South Africa and the Trades Disputes Act Campbell-Bannerman was at his best, on this naval issue he made a grave error likely to endanger the entire safety of the State. And it was very much his responsibility; the imperialist members of the Cabinet had not the power and reputation to carry a stronger defence policy by themselves. The disarmament section, present in the Cabinet, strong in the House and voiced by brilliant journalists and writers, could have been stayed by one man, only by good old C.-B., the genial father, the incorruptible radical, whose writ ran to the further recesses of the radical left.

While on the subject of the Liberal Government's work on defence we may anticipate and ask how its measures stood the actual test of war when it did come in August 1914. It has been commonly asserted that we entered the war "unprepared". This view was natural to Conservatives who had no part in the preparations and who felt, not without reason, that Liberals cared too little for military problems. This belief became very general and the Liberals suffered from it during and at the end of the war in 1918. In the two years of Campbell-Bannerman's rule there was the dangerous relaxation of naval construction and he as Prime Minister was not energetic in supervising defence problems as Chairman of the Committee of Imperial Defence. It should be recollected that he was old, in the last two years of his life, grieved and troubled by his wife's lingering illness which carried her off before him. In any case he had not the natural acumen or the trained professional aptitude that his successor Asquith brought to this task. In the recently published work of Lord Hankey, *The Supreme Command*, we find abundant evidence of Asquith's care and efficiency. His calm and penetrating mind, trained in the severest classical and philosophical disciplines of Oxford, sharpened and enlarged by long practice at the bar and in the business of politics and government, made him a great chairman, not a creator or innovator but one who saw that what had to be done was considered and done by the right men to do it. Lord Hankey, who became secretary of the Committee of Imperial Defence and later of the War Cabinet in 1916, saw the whole process of preparation from the inside and indeed was responsible personally for much that was best in it. Here is his verdict.

"To whom must the credit for this state of affairs belong? First to Balfour, who as Prime Minister had taken the initiative in setting up the Committee of Imperial Defence on a proper footing . . . Next to Asquith, who developed the machine to its fullest capacity, who evolved the policy five years before the emergency and guided the defensive preparations for a war with Germany through all their stages". (Hankey, I, 144.) Sir Robert Ensor in his *Oxford History* emphatically asserts that whatever else may be charged against the Asquith Government want of preparation for war was not one of its faults. Sir Almeric Fitzroy, Clerk to the Privy Council, who had seen the confusion of the beginning of the Boer War, testified in his Diary to the wonderful smoothness of the workings of the government machine in 1914. Sir Julian Corbet, the official historian of the naval operations of the war, concludes:

"Among the many false impressions that prevailed, when after the lapse of a century we found ourselves involved in a great war, not the least erroneous is the belief that we were not prepared for it . . . there is no doubt that the machinery for setting our forces in action had reached an ordered completeness of detail that has no parallel in our history".

And General Edmonds, the official military historian, declares:

"Altogether, Britain never yet entered upon any war with anything approaching such forwardness and forethought in the preparation of the scanty military resources at the disposal of the War Office".

The forethought of the Government extended to many matters, not only the effective mobilisation of the forces on land and sea but also the defence against invasion and all the legal and civilian problems involved, the instructions to shipping, instructions to port authorities to deal with enemy shipping, the rounding up of spies and suspect aliens, arrangements with the Dominions and Colonies. A War Book was edited and kept up to date with instructions for all departments on how to act. Confusion and uncertainty were avoided and clashes between departments foreseen and prevented. The mechanics of preparation could hardly have been more carefully devised. The criticism that can be made against the Liberal Government's defence policy is on broad lines. Our Navy could have been larger and better prepared in various technical ways, docks, mines, submarine defences, armour-piercing shells and other provisions, should have been better. The greater question is the size and strength of the Army. Could the resources at the disposal of the War Office

6

not have been more than the six divisions immediately ready
to enter the battle? Undoubtedly the nation might have
planned for a larger army which would have placed us on a
more equal footing with the continental powers. The
numbers necessary could have been attained only by compulsory service and for this the famous General, Lord Roberts,
vigorously campaigned. He had much sympathy in Conservative circles but the Tory Party never dared to put con-
scription as a policy before the electorate. Moreover within
the Army itself there were objectors to the idea of compulsory
service. It was feared that in the course of the change the
war might strike us with an army in flux and not the smaller
but perfected instrument which we did in fact deploy. Naval
opinion also was hostile to compulsory service, sailors feared
distraction from the primary function of Britain in war, the
power that could promise and maintain the command of the
seas, for itself and for its allies. These matters have been
debated by many learned and expert minds and there is a
large literature on the subject. What cannot be disputed is
that a rational defence policy was planned and fully and
promptly carried out. The pacifist fringe of the party could
not impede Asquith's efforts, the opposition could not show
that they had seriously advocated any fundamental change.
And in this triumph of governmental organisation we may
see the high intellectual qualities of this brilliant Cabinet
working with the élite of the late nineteenth century civil
service and the finest talent of the armed forces. After the war,
in the reaction against the disconcerting brilliance of Lloyd
George, in the long period of the alternations and combination of Baldwin and MacDonald, it became fashionable to
decry too much excellence of mind, to applaud the cosy near-
ness to the common man of agreeable mediocrity. But in the
complexity of modern government there is no substitute for
superior qualities of intellect and strictly disciplined minds
working calmly and unrestingly to order and unravel the
problems which lie before them.

EIGHT

YEARS OF CRISIS

THE YEAR 1908 saw a new Prime Minister and also a dangerous crisis in foreign affairs when Austria by unilateral action annexed Bosnia from the nominal suzerainty of Turkey. The crisis passed with Russia accepting diplomatic defeat. Grey continued with his general policy of seeking peace. This was not done by what was later called appeasement. He was prepared to smooth out all outstanding difficulties with powers where there were problems and sore spots. Russia was the last European power with whom we had been at war and which appeared to have dangerous designs on or near the Indian frontier. Grey's policy was to close the gaps and in 1907 he negotiated a settlement of outstanding differences. This was mainly a matter of defining spheres of influence in Persia, Afghanistan and Tibet. Russia weakened by the Japanese War of 1904 and still more by the revolutionary outbreak of 1905 was willing to negotiate. After this Grey in his quiet unwearied way went on to smooth out sore spots with Germany. These concerned African colonies but still more the scheme which the Germans were furthering as the principal friends of Turkey for a railway which would stretch from opposite Constantinople to the Persian Gulf, the Baghdad railway. In all this, so far as formal agreements went, he succeeded. When the war of 1914 broke out there was actually a convention worked out and initialled awaiting formal ratification by the two governments. However a crisis arose in 1911 when the German Government by sending a warship to Agadir in Morocco seemed to be challenging French interest in that country, an interest fully accepted by Britain in the provisions of what was called the French

Entente. At one time war seemed imminent but Grey made a firm stand. The determination of the Government to stand firm was supported dramatically by Lloyd George, presumed to be a pacifist and opponent of armaments. Speaking at the Mansion House he made it clear in strong words that Britain should at all hazards maintain her place and her prestige among the Great Powers of the world. He would not allow Britain "to be treated as if she were of no account in the Cabinet of nations". The world was impressed by the fact that the most reputedly pacific minister was at one with Asquith and Grey and that the nation would be united.

At this time Foreign policy was not regarded as a party matter. Grey in his election address in 1906 had stated that the parties were in general agreed on foreign policy and had little to tell his constituents of Berwick-on-Tweed on the matter. Foreign policy, to use a modern word, was "bi-partisan". The Unionist opposition respected Grey although their general tendency was to fear that his Liberalism might make him too mild and acquiescent. The Liberals in general admired him but there was always a radical wing who suspected him and many Labour members were prepared to call any war "Capitalist and Imperialist". With the opposition supporting the Government and the division of foreign policy coming well on the left of the Government side Asquith need not fear that on this score his ministry would be in danger. Indeed it was a most unpopular course to criticise Grey and one Liberal who persisted in it was served by his constituency, Coventry, with a warning that he could not be readopted.

While we can now see how European politics were heading towards a catastrophe and while the service chiefs strove ever more earnestly to be ready (Admiral Fisher always predicted a war in 1914 when the Kiel Canal should be enlarged to carry the largest new German Warships), the public in general were not deeply alarmed. But on nearly every other issue of politics there was strife and confusion, and tempers slowly mounted. One of these issues was new and strange and not exactly a party matter. Women were beginning to demand the Parliamentary franchise. The idea was not new. Mill had advocated it in strident terms. But from about 1906 a small and determined group of women worked for the suffrage by violent means. Even at Campbell-Bannerman's first meeting for the election of 1906 at the Albert Hall there had been interruptions. They continued and were always directed against the Government of the day. Parties were split on this issue. Asquith was against votes for women, Grey and Lloyd George for. There were free votes in the House of Commons which showed some Conservative support for the proposal and much Liberal: only the Labour members were united for female suffrage. But as the outrages and illegal acts grew and women were sent to prison by the Courts, which could come to no other verdict on the evidence, the Liberal Ministry suffered loss of face. It was made to seem ridiculous; when it dealt with hunger-striking women in prison by forcible feeding it was made to seem odious. The opposition could not blame the Government; public opinion probably hardened against the "suffragettes" as they were called, but an aura of absurdity and contempt seemed to hang over the Ministry which added to their unpopularity in the more straightforward political struggles which they had to face.

And these were many. We have spoken of years of crisis. The first was a plain constitutional crisis which involved the House of Lords. This arose from the first budget which Lloyd George presented in 1909. It was indeed a remarkable budget worthy to be classed with that of Peel in 1842 and of Gladstone in 1851 and 1861. The Government was under two compulsions for heavy expenditure. One was for social services of which the most notable was the pensions for old people effected in 1909. The other was the need for rapid expanse of the Navy. Both had to be admitted; if Naval expenditure was not raised the Government would be at the mercy of its enemies. If social service expenditure was not raised it would be betraying its radical mission. To meet both needs about fifteen million extra had to be raised, an increase of about a tenth. From this point it may be said that the Liberals had to abandon the old slogan "retrenchment". The word was still heard but no one believed it. The budget of 1909, styled by its author "the People's Budget", had important elements which were not political such as the beginning of funds for roads, forestry and other developments. It had one old Liberal specific, increased taxes on drink, which were as usual unpopular. But the main element in the budget which made it a social-democratic measure was that it set out as never before to tax the rich (the expression "soak the rich" was not then in common use). Income tax was raised, and that spares the very poorest, and death duties were sharply increased on all but the smallest estates. And an entirely new and discriminatory impost, called supertax (now surtax), was levied on holders of incomes over £3000 who would then be distinctly wealthy people. All this was legislation for the masses against the classes. But Lloyd Goerge went further and proposed a tax on the class of classes, on the landlords, the most envied and hated grade of society in radical eyes. This was a tax of 20 per cent on the increased value of land levied if it were sold, to be more accurate on the "unearned increment of land", on that which arose by the general wealth of the community as opposed to the efforts of the landlord to improve his land. It was complex and cumbrous but it revived the spirits of the followers of Henry George, the "single-taxers", and it seemed to have on its side an argument from social equity. On this tax the opposition centred as its author desired and intended. Of course not all landowners are lords and dukes. It would hit many a humble owner and many a seedy speculator. But when the landed interest grew hot in their opposition Lloyd George aimed at the highest heads and the folly of the Lords in rejecting the Finance Bill gave him his chance. In a famous speech in Limehouse he attacked the high aristocracy, dukes who cost as much as dreadnoughts, the fortunate eldest sons and heirs, "the first of the litter". On the plane of sheer class demagogy he aroused radical enthusiasm.

But the action of the Lords in throwing out the Finance Bill of the year gave Asquith his chance too. The action was legal, but according to all the known precedents of constitutional life it was a breach of ancient custom. From the seventeenth and eighteenth centuries precedents could be quoted. Gladstone in 1861 had sent up the first complete finance Bill to the Lords defying them to reject it and they had given in. Nothing could have been more apt for the learned and majestic oratory of the great Liberal lawyer than this. He was now at the height of his powers and his performance in leading the party on the House of Lords question was the most perfect of his distinguished career. He and Lloyd George were like a pair of batsmen in partnership, the one a perfect stylist, the other a punishing forcing batsman knocking the bowlers off their length. Two general elections were necessary to settle the crisis. The first in January 1910 followed the rejection of the budget. The second in December 1910 followed an attempt by the party leaders to reach a compromise after the death of King Edward VII, a genuine effort to ease the path of the young King George V. These two elections were perhaps the only occasions on which the people of Britain had the question put to them, Do you wish to become a full democracy? The basis of the Liberal case was that, if the Lords could at will destroy Liberal projects and always accept Conservative proposals, political justice did not exist. Their solution, a moderate solution, was to make it illegal for the Lords to reject any finance Bill and to make any other Bill become law after it had been passed three times by the Commons in three sessions extending over more than two years. This was enacted in the Parliament Act of 1911 and a further act of 1949 has reduced the period of delay to one year. We accept it readily enough. What has to be remembered is the reason for the extreme bitterness of this dispute in the period 1909 to 1911. It went very deep. Behind the Liberal proposals was the idea that the Constitution was not fixed and could not be fixed. The will of the electorate as shown by the House of Commons and sustained must prevail. The Conservative idea was that there was some basic element in the constitution, some check to extreme democracy and that this was vested in the Lords who could not indeed oppose for ever but might reasonably delay for a long period the carrying of a radical reform. And what radical reform might be carried that would in reality "subvert" the constitution? Everyone knew the answer. One element in the constitution that must not be tampered with was the Union, the glorious fruit of the centuries, which had made Scotland, England and Ireland and Wales one realm, one indivisible polity. Unless there could be a guarantee that such a step could not be brought within the realm of possibility the Conservatives would yield to no reform of the Lords. They had two means of resistance but both failed them. They had hopes that the great Radical majority of 1906 would melt away. It melted indeed but not altogether away. The first election of 1910 gave the Government a majority of 124. The second showed a majority of 126. The people would not change their minds: Parliament had now to act. The second hope of the Conservatives was that the Government could not carry its reform of the Lords, the removal of the legislative veto over the sustained opposition of the Peers. Only one resort is provided in the Constitution for such a deadlock. It had been threatened in 1832 to carry the Reform Bill. The King could create Peers by prerogative act without limit. The Conservatives hoped in the first place that Asquith would not have the face to ask for it and in the second place that the King would refuse. They were wrong. The indignation of the radical side in politics was deep and strong; the Liberals had no hesitation in asking George V for the remedy that William IV had provided. Before the election of December 1910 Asquith had privately secured from the King a promise that, if needed, such peers would be created. It would have needed over four hundred. This would be awkward; it would even be absurd. But the Liberals were in a mood to be awkward and it was the Lords who would look absurd. In the early session of 1911 a Parliament Bill was brought in and in August it reached the statute book by a narrow majority of nineteen for the Third Reading in the Lords. Even at the last moment the King had to send his Private Secretary, Lord Knollys, to assure doubting peers that the threat of creation was real.

Now to understand the extreme political bitterness of the next few years it is necessary to understand that on the Conservative side it was felt that the Liberals' act in forcing the King, "playing the bully in the royal closet" put them morally out of court. They had, it was alleged, "abused the constitution". The Opposition therefore had a moral right to use more than ordinary methods in their conduct of politics. It was also pointed out that the majority of the House of Commons that had perpetuated the "outrage" of the Parliament Act was not a majority of Liberals over Conservatives; these two parties were in fact equal, 272 Conservatives and Unionists to 272 Liberals. The majority was made up by 42 Labour and 84 Nationalists. To the Tory mind this carried little conviction. The Nationalists were by their nature disloyal, rebel at heart, only concerned for their own ends, Home Rule and thereafter independence. The Labour members also were felt to be persons with no sense of imperial responsibility, demagogues, socialists, levellers. The Liberal Government, it was alleged, was a prisoner of the Irish leader, Redmond, and must do all his bidding. And the distribution of the representation was not without significance. In England the Unionists had 241 seats, the Government only 223. It was from Wales, 31 Radical to 3 Unionist and from Scotland, 61 Radical to 9 Unionist that the Government

6*

drew its preponderant strength, the Celtic fringe.[1] A sense of desperation began to fill the Conservatives' minds. They felt themselves to be living in a revolutionary period in which the true heart of the English people if touched would in the end see the right. One of their leaders, the stately Wiltshire squire Walter Long, declared in a speech that he was not one to stand idly by while a revolution was in progress. He was taken up by G. K. Chesterton in a brilliant satirical poem:

> "It suffers but it may not suffer wrong,
> It suffers but it cannot suffer Long.
> Walter be wise, avoid the wild and new,
> The Constitution is the thing for you."

It is significant that the last motion to carry the Parliament Act in the House of Commons was the occasion of a scene of disorder leading to the Speaker adjourning the House and led by two Noble Members, Lord Hugh Cecil and Lord Winterton.

With the Parliament Act on the statute book one crisis was over but it left bitter memories. From now on party antagonisms were deeper and the Unionists began to feel that with the Constitution rigged against them, as they thought, they had a moral right to overstep the normal bounds of opposition. Social intercourse between Liberals and Conservatives in London Society became difficult. Another crisis that arose was equally disturbing both to the Government and the Conservative opposition. In many branches of industry the workers were passing into open revolt. During the years, 1911, 1912 there were numerous

---

[1] London was about equally divided, 30 Unionists to 29 Radicals. In the Southern Counties of England there were 104 Unionists to 51 Radicals, in the Midlands 50 to 38, and it was only in industrial Northern England that the Unionists were in a minority, 50 to 104 Radicals. The University Members, all Unionist, are not included in these regional figures.

strikes. On the political front the Labour movement was dissatisfied. They had only 40 seats in Parliament and many of these were only held by the grace of the middle class Liberals in not offering a candidate. It was difficult to support candidates when elected. Some Trade Unions did make a levy on their members for Labour Party purposes but a case known as the Osborne Case was brought before the courts and it was held and upheld on appeal in 1909 that such a levy was illegal. The most powerful instrument for promoting Labour men in politics was struck from their hand. The Liberal Government came to the rescue by providing for payment of members which had for long been vaguely on their programme. An Act of 1913 authorised the Unions to have political funds from which members could contract out but unless they did so they paid the levy. Many Liberals and most Conservatives felt that this was a dangerous concession.

We have not space even to enumerate the many strikes which took place from 1910 onwards. In 1910 a railway strike in the North East. Later a lock-out by employers in the cotton industry, and a fourteen weeks' lock-out in the boilermaking industry. There was a violent and riotous strike in the South Wales coal-field and troops were used to restore order. In 1911 the Port of London was paralysed and other ports disturbed. In August 1911 there was a railway strike covering the greater part of England. In 1912 the coal miners came out for a national minimum wage and nearly a million men withdrew their labour. Asquith met the problem by passing an Act for district minimum wage machinery. After this there was something of a lull but shortly before war broke out, Sir George Askwith, the chief of the Labour Department of the Board of Trade (the forerunner of the present Ministry of Labour), feared that there would be worse trouble than ever before in the industrial world. The outbreak of war made it impossible to verify this prediction. Some of these disputes were regular fights for better wages but there was present also the spirit of continental syndicalism. This implies direct action by the workers to secure their economic and political aims: it regarded the trade unions as the basic political organism of a worker's polity with no moral obligation to the laws, forms and authority of "the bourgeois state". Its ideal culmination was the general strike of all workers. This was threatened in France, had occurred in Sweden and took place in Britain in 1926.

In the face of all this what could a government, a Liberal government, do? In an interesting book, *The Strange Death of Liberal England*, Mr. G. Dangerfield has painted a picture of these times which presents Asquith and his colleagues as men moving impotently as in a dream, either unconscious of the terrible forces which played about them or unable to act to meet the peril. It may be true that Englishmen in general and Liberals in particular were slow to appreciate the forces that were shaking society. Looking back now we can see that the shadows of this dreadful century of violence and terror were falling upon Europe. It may even be said that Asquith was over-optimistic, with the calm efficiency of a not very imaginative man. But the Liberal Government had its policy and its philosophy for dealing with the social and socialist problem. They were not without remedies for some of the more glaring social evils. In 1909 the young Winston Churchill at the Board of Trade passed an act limiting hours of work in mines to eight hours. In the same year a Trade Boards Act was passed to regulate and improve wages and conditions among the workers in homes and very small work-shops where poverty and grinding toil were worst. This was later extended to many employments. From 1909 to 1911 the Government was out of action in the House of Lords over the budget dispute and fought two general elections. But when that was over they returned to social reform with the famous National Insurance Act which provided insurance for the lower income groups against both sickness and unemployment. The Labour Exchanges set up by Churchill in 1909 were used to administer it. The Act failed to please the true socialists, for it was contributory, the employee, the employer and the state all paid a share. Lloyd George, who carried it as Chancellor, performed remarkable feats of negotiations with the medical profession who at first opposed it and with the Unions and Friendly Societies who were called in to assist in the operation of the Act. Here, and later as a conciliator in strikes, Lloyd Goerge showed himself to be a man of most extraordinary gifts with the power to enlighten, to explain and to bring together in agreement the most hostile and stubborn of opposing interests. Before, through and after the war he displayed again and again this almost magic power. His last effort was his greatest, the Irish Treaty of 1921. Liberals have claimed and still claim that the Insurance Act of 1911 marks beyond all other events the birth of the Welfare State. The Labour party naturally prefers the date 1945. It is a matter of degree, like a dispute as to whether the egg or the chicken is the most important.

The Conservatives at first seemed not unfriendly to the Bill when it was first introduced, for they had a tradition of social reform from Disraeli's day. But as the long debate went on and they saw the hated Welsh demagogue ever more the master of the field their ire rose. Moreover the Bill touched many interests and aroused much natural hostility. It must be remembered that the many bureaucratic forms which we now have to accept, and the many little acts of cooperation with some government agency that we are now accustomed to, were then practically unknown. The 1914 war with its registrations and rationing conditioned the nation to complying with the minor commands of government. There must be few kitchen dressers or living-room cupboards now which have not their pile of insurance cards, medical cards, etc. Then it did seem to be an outrage and an imposition. And by whom was it ordered? Not by the King or the realm but by Lloyd George, the odious little solicitor of Criccieth. It was too much. Opposition swelled to fantastic heights, even at the time to thinking men the complaints were ridiculous. Now they seem grotesque. The inauguration of the first and greatest scheme for insulating the destitute and sick amongst the labouring poor from the worst vicissitudes of life was described as "licking stamps for Lloyd George".

To understand the position of the Liberal party in these stormy years it is necessary to pass a judgment on the characteristics of the Conservatives at this time. Such a judgment must be suspect of being partisan. But the conduct of the Conservatives or Unionists at this time was so marked by inordinate anger and contempt, so haughty and so intolerant of their opponents, so convinced of their mission and their right to rule the Empire and the kingdom as the only persons sufficiently loyal and true-hearted to fulfil this task, that they seem to be touched with that moral disease which Roman authors described by the word "superbia", overweening pride. And when we read Mr. Dangerfield's account of the somnambulist trance of the Liberal Ministers we should ask the hypothetical question, what would the Unionists have done if they had had charge of the Government in these years of social discontent, of hatred and violence on the part of the workers, with women going to prison for their rights, with Irish nationalism denied all hope of self-government moving rapidly to open republicanism? If the attitude of the Conservative party was in doubt, and there is little sign that it was, a decisive change was made when in 1912 Balfour resigned under pressure from a party defeated in three successive elections. In his place Bonar Law was chosen as leader. Bonar Law was no typical Tory. He was the son of a Presbyterian minister in Canada who had been brought as a boy to the West of Scotland where he inherited a fortune and became a successful iron merchant. He was elected to give more ginger to the party, to give no ground to the hated radicals. As well as Scottish he had Ulster ante-cedents and from the end of 1912 Ulster became the main problem in politics. The social question was acute, the labour situation alarming. War threatened as an ever present danger. During the Agadir crisis of 1911 many precautionary measures had been taken, squadrons alerted, bridges guarded. But it was the Irish and Ulster question that grew larger and more menacing. Here there was a threat of disobedience to the legal government, a refusal to accept the commands of the King's Ministers, those who had kissed hands and received the seals of office, who were supported with regular approval by large majorities by the Commons of the realm in Parliament assembled. And the bearers of this challenge were not the confused, suffering and fiery socialists of East London or Liverpool, of South Wales or Glasgow. They were the highest and noblest in the land, men of wealth, rank and education, holders of His Majesty's Commission in the armed forces, Members of the most honourable Privy Council. It seemed that we were back in 1641, the time when our politics began. Was Rupert to ride again?

The unity of the realm was threatened by faction. But who were the factious, the high-born and wealthy with their numerous supporters far down the social scale who were ready to defy the established government? Or were they the smooth-tongued Ministers who were in power by demagogic arts and the corrupt support of rebel Irish and the insurgent elements of the working class? That was the question at issue. We must see how the Liberals faced this, to them, most surprising and almost incredible challenge and assault.

Since 1886 the Liberal Party, shorn of its unionist elements, had carried Home Rule on its banner. It was pressed with varying degrees of ardour or faintheartedness by different persons at different times. It was clear enough at the elections of 1910 that a Liberal Government would proceed to enact a Home Rule Bill for Ireland, but admittedly it came rather low on the bill, the Lords, the Budget and Free Trade being more popular items. The Unionists asked sarcastically why when the Liberals had a huge independent majority in 1906 they did not then proceed to put through Home Rule? To this there was a good answer. It was useless painfully to put through a complicated Bill which the Lords would certainly throw out. If the Lords strained at comparatively harmless gnats like Licensing Bills, Bills to abolish Plural Voting or encourage Scottish small-holders, it was certain that they would impose a veto on Home Rule for Ireland. When the Parliament Act was on the statute book the way was clear. But now the Liberal majority had shrunk and the Irish Nationalist Party with its 84 members held the balance. They had faithfully delivered the Irish vote at the elections to Liberal and Labour candidates. There was no excuse for further delay. But this dependence on the Irish, on "King Redmond" as he was called, did lose the Liberals some moral credit. Unionists were inclined to feel, half-charitably, that only this political duress could explain why at least the better sort of Liberal could bring himself to "break up the Empire" and dissolve the unity of the United Kingdom.

The Bill was duly brought in at the beginning of the session of 1912. At the same time a Bill to disestablish the Welsh Church was brought forward. It received the Royal Assent under the Parliament Act, like the Home Rule Bill, but unlike it was actually carried into operation in 1919–20. The Home Rule Bill was on the lines of Gladstone's Bill of 1893. It provided for a moderate measure of self-government reserving Imperial matters, defence, customs and foreign policy to the Parliament at Westminster in which the Irish were to have a reduced number of representatives 42 instead of 104. It seems a mild enough measure now when we consider that in 1921 Ireland was given full dominion status, minus the six counties. Still more does it seem mild when we observe how African colonies are ushered into full independence with presents of maces and speakers' chairs and members of the Royal Family to grace the event. But some things must be remembered. The mere fact of conceding Home Rule was seen by the Imperialists as the beginning of a rot. It would encourage Indian and other dissident subjects of the King-Emperor. It was foreboded that the Irish would not be content with this half-loaf but would move to greater independence, and it was assumed as a matter of strategy that Britain dare not fight a war without full military control of Ireland. Then there was the question of obligation to those Irishmen who did not want Home Rule, about a quarter of the whole, the Protestants of Ulster and the more thinly spread Protestants of the rest of Ireland, the "loyalists", those who served the Crown and the state all over the world, or had courageously endured in their own country the outrages of the rebels, intimidation, boycott, rent strikes, cattle-maiming, assault and murder. Were they to be handed over to the tyranny of papist peasants, in all ways by which sensible men could judge, their inferiors?

As the Bill passed its weary way through Parliament in 1912 and 1913 some things began to be clear. It appeared that the Unionist case against Home Rule for the larger part of Ireland was weakening. In the Dominions which had achieved full self-government there was not the same apprehension as in England. In America opinion was unanimously in favour, whether Anglophobe or Anglophile. The Unionists did not weaken in their general opposition but by the end of 1913 they were tending to retreat into the Keep of the Castle, into Belfast and Ulster.[1]

The famous Dublin lawyer, Sir Edward Carson, was invited North to head a movement of resistance and with the help of the able and determined Protestants of Belfast he

[1] The word Ulster is convenient. Actually the Province of Ulster consists of nine counties. Four of these, Londonderry, Antrim, Down and Armagh, are predominantly Protestant. Two, Tyrone and Fermanagh, have a small Catholic majority. Three, Donegal, Cavan and Monaghan, are mainly Catholic and were included in the Free State, now the Irish Republic. In Belfast there is a considerable Catholic minority which was able in one division to return a Nationalist, Mr. Devlin, before 1914 and even after. The other three provinces of Ireland, Leinster, Munster and Connaught, are overwhelmingly Catholic and Nationalist.

made preparations for a "Provisional Government" which would take over, if the infamy of a Dublin Parliament was imposed. This was a serious movement. These people meant what they said and showed it by their actions. They subscribed to a "Covenant"; the ancient biblical term was used with all its emotional appeal to those of Presbyterian strain. They organised in units, they drilled, they arranged to import arms and did so successfully. From England came words of encouragement. Bonar Law, the Unionist leader, could see no lengths of resistance in which they would not be justified. They lacked nothing in support in the Army, and at the War Office, Henry Wilson, Director of military operations and later in 1918 Chief of the General Staff, freely supplied them with information.

Now Asquith and his colleagues were aware from the first that Ulster would be a problem. How great a problem none of them perhaps realised and Asquith least of all. But we know that they did discuss, when the Bill was first presented, whether they should include some reasonable concession to Ulster. They decided to wait. For this there was one good reason. If the Bill was presented in a form unsatisfactory to Redmond and the Irish it would fail in its intended effect of conciliating Ireland. Amendment later might be necessary. But now we are coming to a moment when the counting of heads at Westminster or in the constituencies was no longer the root of the matter. It was becoming a matter of force and of the intensity of opinion that will drive men to the use of force. Middle class professional Liberals were not inclined to think in terms of force. Just as they were taken aback by the furious violence of the women suffragists and of the syndicalist socialists, so they failed to realise that the English aristocracy were strong-tempered men, men whose preferred occupation was service in arms, men who could endure much in a democratic age but whose patience with demagogues and silver-tongued lawyers was wearing thin.

And the Liberals knew very little of Belfast and Ulster. A

generation had passed since any Liberal member had come from there. There was a long tradition of insurgence amongst the Ulster Protestants who could speak of "kicking the King's Crown into the Boyne", and a respectable Belfast paper printed, and a few years ago was still printing on its front page heading, the Latin motto, "*pro rege saepe, pro patria semper*". And Ulster, Protestant Ulster, although it does not indulge in the attitudes of left-wing nationalism is and remains a "*patria*", something for which it is sweet and decorous to die. There was thus in prospect a trial of strength of a kind that British politicians had not known for generations or indeed centuries. Professor George O'Brien of Dublin has stated in an interesting study, *The Four Green Fields*, that at this time there were three powers in Ireland, the power of the British Crown, the power of Irish Nationalism, the power of the Orange Order in Ulster. And he concludes that the third power proved in the end the strongest.

The story of the Irish crisis in these years has a large literature. Space is lacking to trace the events which are well described by Halévy, Ensor and others. A recent book by Mr. A. P. Ryan, *Mutiny at the Curragh*, has given a good description of that, the central event of the crisis. We are here concerned not with a judgment on the rights and wrongs of the whole problem but with understanding the Liberal approach. Asquith's handling of the situation has frequently been denounced. Ensor calls it weak. Halévy refrains from judgment but leaves no doubt about its ineffectiveness. Asquith's biographer, the late Mr. J. A. Spender, in his book *The Public Life* with great skill gives the case for Asquith's policy of delay and mildness in the face of what was technically rebellion and sedition. The basis of this case is that Redmond himself was eager for a quiet settlement. He wanted Irish Home Rule to dawn "under the star of peace". It may fairly be said that Asquith can be accused of unprospectiveness. He seems to have lacked foresight and imagination. Even in July 1914 Archbishop Davidson returned from a conference with the Prime Minister appalled at the fact that even then he did not seem to know how bad things were. Others of his colleagues, it is known, saw further. Both Lloyd George and Churchill were anxious at an earlier stage, both were more flexible in their ideas for conciliation and Churchill at any rate more zealous for active suppression of the Ulstermen.

As the situation grew worse there were some private talks between Asquith and Bonar Law but without result. The trouble ran on until by 1914 the Ulstermen seemed fully organised and in the South an Irish National Volunteer movement was organised and both were drilling hard. That the Ulstermen in April 1914 succeeded in running German guns at Larne while in July the Irish volunteers failed at Howth made matters much worse. But the centre of the crisis lay in the question, could the Liberal Government rely on the Army?

We have already seen that the Liberal elements in the Army were very weak. It was not their form of life. Most commissioned officers could be safely regarded as Unionists. Many were Irish Protestants including some of the most distinguished.[1]

[1] Of feeling in the Navy very little has appeared. The Navy was strenuously at work preparing for the war which they rightly thought to be imminent, and their horror of anything savouring of disobedience was deep rooted. Naval memoirs reveal that the future Admiral Lord Keyes, who was then on submarine work at the Admiralty, endangered his career by his open detestation of the First Lord, Winston Churchill: Admiral Usborne reveals in his memoirs that in March 1914 his ship was stationed in Lamlash Bay, Arran, and they had orders to ship field guns to take to Belfast. His Captain asked him that evening what he would do if he had to act against Ulster? Usborne replied that he supposed he would obey the legal Government. The Captain, unnamed, replied that he would resign his commission. Commander Sir Stephen King-Hall tells us in his memoirs that at this time the officers of his ship were summoned by Commodore Goodenough, later to be famous at the Battle of Jutland, and told that if any orders came they had to be obeyed and that was that.

Service as an officer in the British Army was at that time a profession with severe requirements; many laboured hard whether at the regimental or the staff level to perfect themselves in their duties. It was no mere parade ground activity. The chances of action on the Indian frontier or elsewhere were good and most officers of more than twelve years seniority had seen active service in Africa. But the Army was also an avocation or occupation for men of rank and family, very honourable and proper. Enlisted men served for a period of years and if they left without an agreed discharge they were deserters. Officers received commissions but they were usually permitted to resign them when they chose. Their obedience was implicit; they were English gentlemen who by definition could not be disloyal.

Many of the wealthier and well-born officers tended to serve in the cavalry and it was amongst cavalry officers stationed at the Curragh in Central Ireland that trouble broke out. The Government, as a reasonable precaution, proposed to move troops into the Belfast region to safeguard depots and stores. The Commander-in-chief in Ireland handled the matter unwisely. Instead of giving such orders as were needed he told the officers where they were to go and indicated that those whose homes were in Ulster might be excused from this particular duty. In the end fifty-eight officers stated that they would prefer to resign rather than take action against Ulster. In a telegram to the War Office their commander, General Gough, used the words that "they would prefer to accept dismissal if ordered north". This meant that they would be willing to sacrifice their military careers and accept the ignominy of dismissal in a cause that seemed to them to be that of political honour. This event was called "the Mutiny at the Curragh". It was not precisely mutiny, for no one disobeyed an order given. But it had all the effects of a mutiny. The War Minister, Seeley, was compelled to resign after issuing a document which was too conciliatory to the offending officers. The situation was that the army, the instrument for keeping order in Ireland, was breaking in the Prime Minister's hand. Radical opinion flared up violently. The Commons were told by Labour Members that if officers could refuse to carry out the Government's policy the soldiers could refuse to intervene in strikes. The cry was raised, "The Army versus the People." The normal constitutional processes were failing. Asquith's response was to take strong action but strictly within parliamentary forms. He decided to take the Army in his hands and became Secretary of War himself, vacated his seat and was re-elected and until August 1914 he ran both the War Office and the Cabinet. The only alternative was a dissolution and an election which if it had resulted in a Liberal victory (and perhaps it was their best chance), would give the Government full authority to command obedience in the forces. The result would have been doubtful, the decision would have been rash. And yet it is possible to argue that it would have been right. So far as Ireland was concerned the results of inaction were utterly deplorable. It was felt that there was one law for the Green and another for the Orange. Nationalist Irish rebellions were met with crimes acts, coercion acts, suspension of habeas corpus, strengthened garrisons and well-disposed machine guns. When Protestants revolted it needed but one blast of the Unionist trumpet and the walls of Jericho would fall. Many young Irishmen at this moment turned away from Parliamentary methods to preparing open rebellion.[1]

But in Asquith's defence it must be remembered that there are more problems in politics than the problem of Ireland. Europe was in an uncertain state. The storm was not yet ready to break but under a dull sky there were fitful breezes rustling the grass and stirring the branches of the trees. It was a hard time to rule an Empire. A responsible statesman must have doubted whether the way of safety was to force a

[1] Including the present President of the Irish Republic, Mr. de Valera. The author has heard this from his own lips in an interview in Dublin.

bitter election between the radical parties and the Army. As Burke has wisely said, in government there is very commonly only a choice between evil and evil.

A final effort to settle the Ulster question was made at a conference called by the King at Buckingham Palace. Even that failed. With the coming of war the problem was shelved, shelved but not solved. The next important event of Irish history was the rebellion of April 1916 in Dublin. It may be said that the Liberals failed in this crisis because they had not learned, like Walpole, to "act within the limits of the possible". They should have known that Ulster could not be coerced and that the people of England, or a sufficient number of them, would see that she was not coerced. Asquith should have realised that he was no de Gaulle, that his ship could not weather the storm. It may be so. It can certainly be argued that the ministry was at fault in not asking, long before, the question of how Ulster could be controlled, what preparatory measures should be taken, who the most suitable officers and units would be to employ? This would have been wise[1] but it is not certain that it would have been effective. No move could have been kept secret and all would have been suspected. Even the modest move to strengthen the garrison of Ulster in March 1914 was denounced by Mr. Amery and many other Unionist members as "a plot", while Churchill's assembling of a fleet in Lamlash Bay earned him the most bitter enmity and had much to do with driving him from the Admiralty in 1915. But if Ulster could not be made to bow to the will of Parliament, the rest of Ireland could not be conciliated. This was the consequence of Asquith's failure. But was it his failure, or was it the failure of the English people years before to hearken to the voice of the great

[1] Mr. Ryan in his book on the Curragh suggests that if the Commander in Ireland, General Paget, had been less flamboyant and indiscreet and if the commander of the infantry, General Fergusson (afterwards a distinguished Corps Commander in the war), had been in charge, he might have handled the situation.

Gladstone when he called upon them to make an act of restitution, a sacrifice of their complacency and pride before a nation which by the general testimony of mankind they had neglected and oppressed? Ireland in the end won its freedom and Ulster its adherence to Great Britain. Ireland remains divided like the Netherlands, like India, modern Germany and many other lands, for geography is not all, and religion, race, differing faiths and cultures, impose their barriers on the face of the earth.

The year 1914 found the Liberal party in low water. It was suffering in public esteem. It was losing by-elections, even such strongholds as Leith and Midlothian. Lloyd George and some of his colleagues had offended against strict ministerial morality by investing in Marconi Wireless, shares in an American company with the knowledge that the Government was about to contract with the British Marconi company and this would raise the shares of its corresponding ally overseas. A committee of the House investigated this "scandal"; the majority whitewashed, the minority condemned. Also Lloyd George's insurance act was successfully brought into force, a great administrative achievement, but the public disliked it, especially the poorest workers for whom it was most needed. They had been told that for their contribution of fourpence they would receive ninepence. But they saw the fourpence gone and the ninepence seemed a bird in the bush. If peace had been kept and if the Government had somehow survived the Ulster crisis, Parliament was due for dissolution in 1915. Every omen suggested that it would lead to a great unionist victory. The Labour Party were talking of putting up 200 candidates, mostly in radical seats, and this alone would probably have put the Unionists in power even if there had been no general swing in their favour, as by every sign there was. Even without the war the radical movement, by which is meant the anti-conservative forces in the country, was in schism and this schism has kept Conservatism in power for all but nine of the last forty years.

The onrush of the war in late July and the first four days of August put strains on Liberal unity but it was maintained. At one time it seemed as though some members, even including Lloyd George, would resign if the occasion of the war was only our obligation to France. This was not a binding treaty and the military conversations which Campbell-Bannerman had permitted with the French in January 1906 were not known to many members of the Cabinet until 1912. The problem was solved by the German invasion of Belgium which raised a specific treaty obligation, an obligation which Gladstone had been ready to observe in 1870. So with only the resignation of the elderly radicals, Lord Morley and John Burns, the Cabinet entered into the war as a unit. The calm and efficient conduct of Asquith and Grey at this crisis roused wide public admiration and for a time it could be said that they never stood so high in the general opinion of the nation.

Strains and difficulties developed as the war went on. No British Prime Minister who has been in office at the beginning of a general war has remained in office to the end. The Government as constituted by Asquith remained in being until May 1915 when criticism over the unsuccessful attempt to capture Gallipoli, the resignation of Lord Fisher as First Sea Lord and complaints about inadequate provision of shells compelled Asquith to seek a coalition with the Conservatives. Eighteen months later this administration fell from internal disputes about the best mode of organising the direction of the war. This began the famous and ruinous schism in the Liberal Party. It is still a matter of controversy. One point of view put forward by Asquith's friends is that it was a treacherous and unnecessary move by Lloyd George to seize the Prime Ministership. But this crisis must not be judged as an essay in the ethics of political friendship. There were terrible issues at stake. There was a war to be won—or lost. By what system and by what man could we best be governed? There was at issue a deep question of the organisation of the Cabinet for the direction of the war. There are those still who think that Asquith with his calm, orthodox mind, his belief in good professional advice and well tried methods, was better than Lloyd George's brilliant and impatient plans which made him a plague to Generals and Admirals. There are those who think that he did well to be a plague to Generals and Admirals and that both by his system, the War Cabinet of five or six men, and by his energetic personality he and he alone could have saved the country. Even now evidence is still coming out and judgments are being revised. We have already cited a judgment of the man who most continuously sat in the centre of the war machine, Lord Hankey. In his book he is deeply respectful to both great Liberal statesmen. Later in 1923 Asquith and Lloyd George were to know a brief reconciliation. But it was not deep seated and the reconciliation did not last. The words of the poet Coleridge may stand as an epitaph of this most fruitful but tragically broken alliance of the two finest minds of modern Liberalism.

> Alas! they had been friends in youth;
> But whispering tongues can poison truth;
>
> Each spake words of high disdain
> And insult to his heart's best brother;
>
> A dreary sea now flows between,
> But neither heat, nor frost, nor thunder,
> Shall wholly do away, I ween,
> The marks of that which once hath been.

SUGGESTIONS FOR FURTHER READING

THE GENERAL HISTORY of the period can be studied in the two volumes of the Oxford History of England:

Woodward E. L. The Age of Reform.
Ensor R. C. K. England 1870 to 1914.
and in Trevelyan G. M. England in the Nineteenth Century.

A full and illuminating history is to be found in Halévy E. History of the English People in the Nineteenth Century, Volumes I, II, III, and IV, covering from 1815 to 1852; Volumes V and VI from 1895 to 1914.

A full and interesting account of the earlier and middle parts of the century is to be found in Walpole, Spencer, History of England from the conclusion of the Great War in 1815 to 1856, followed by History of Twenty-Five Years (1856–1880) which gives the views of a near contemporary.

Jennings W. I. in a recent work, Party Politics, Volume I., Appeal to the People and Volume II The Growth of Parties gives an excellent account of the development of Parties and their relation to public opinion.

Hanham H. J. Elections and Party Management, 1959, gives a detailed study of party organisation and its problems.

There is a wealth of biographical literature from which the following may be cited:

Eyck E. Life of Gladstone.
Morley J. Life of Gladstone. 1903.
Morley J. Life of Cobden. 1879.
Guedalla P. Life of Palmerston.
Trevelyan G. O. Life of Macaulay. 1876.

Trevelyan G. M. Life of Bright. 1913.

Gardiner A. G. Life of Harcourt. 1923.

Garvin J. L. and Amery, Julian, Life of Joseph Chamberlain, Volume I. 1932.

Spender J. A. and Asquith C. Life of Lord Oxford and Asquith. 1932.

Grey of Falloden. Twenty-Five Years. 1925.

Haldane Viscount. An Autobiography.

Jones T. Life of Lloyd George. 1951.

On the connection between Liberalism and the radical movement, Maccoby S. English Radicalism. 1832–1852.

On the all important Irish problem there is Hammond J. L., Gladstone and The Irish Nation, 1938, and also Mansergh, N. Ireland in the Age of Reform and Revolution, 1940.

Bullock, Alan, and Shock, Maurice, The Liberal Tradition from Fox to Keynes is a most valuable collection of extracts from Liberal thinkers and statesmen.

INDEX